T0361709

TO:

....

FROM:

....

DATE:

....

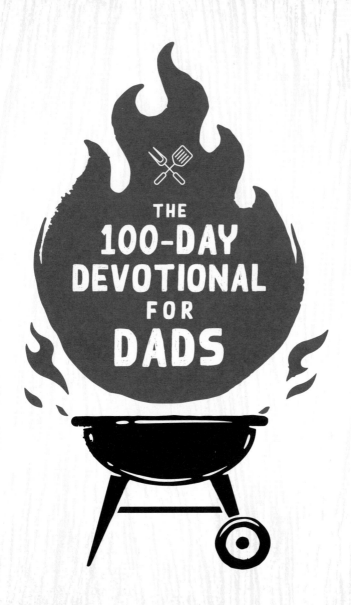

THE
100-DAY
DEVOTIONAL
FOR
DADS

THE
100-DAY
DEVOTIONAL
FOR
DADS

BARBOUR
PUBLISHING

Written by Dwight Clough and Paul Kent.

ISBN 979-8-89151-045-6

Published by Barbour Publishing, Inc., 1810 Barbour Drive, Uhrichsville, Ohio 44683, www.barbourbooks.com

Our mission is to inspire the world with the life-changing message of the Bible.

Member of the
Evangelical Christian
Publishers Association

Printed in China.

THE PERFECT WAY TO SPEND THE NEXT HUNDRED DAYS. . .

The 100-Day Devotional for Dads offers relatable, real-life wisdom and inspiration for everyday living. Fathers, you'll encounter page after page of biblical truths that you can apply to every area of your life, no matter how old your kids are.

This book covers all the key topics that dads face on a daily basis:

- Family
- Courage
- Culture
- Stress
- Wisdom
- Priorities
- Strength
- and much more

Each reading is complemented by a carefully selected scripture selection and short prayer-starter. These devotions encourage you to spend time in your heavenly Father's presence so that you can become the dad your kids need you to be.

The 100-Day Devotional for Dads is the perfect way for every father to spend his next one hundred days!

A GIFT FROM GOD

Children are a gift from the LORD;
they are a reward from him.
PSALM 127:3 NLT

It could have been the other way around: our children could have been the parents, and we could have been the children. We could have been born at a later moment in time, and then we would need to answer to our kids instead of our children answering to us. We dads know this. Why exactly each of us was given the parents we were given and the children we have is a mystery that we may not fully understand in this life. But we believe we were put here for a reason—in this exact moment in history, in this family, with these children.

We are doing God's work. We are raising His children. No, our children don't belong to us. But yes, we are responsible for them. Parenting is a sacred trust. The moment we become dads, our lives are forever changed. We have taken on a task of eternal significance. We have brought new life into the world, and we have taken on responsibility for nurturing and protecting it.

A newborn baby, a running and laughing child, an ambivalent teen, a young adult testing her wings, the father of our grandchildren, the hands that will close our eyes on this life, the faces we will someday greet from our home in heaven—fatherhood takes us through many seasons, some filled with joy, others riddled with pain.

But we are never alone on this journey. We have a Father in heaven who walks with us as we change diapers, read bedtime stories, wait up past curfew, look for that phone call, offer our parting words of advice. To Him we commit our imperfect efforts to be good fathers to our precious children. In the end, we leave the results with Him.

GOD, WHAT AN HONOR IT IS TO BE A DAD TO THE CHILDREN YOU HAVE ENTRUSTED TO MY CARE. YOU KNOW THAT I COULD NEVER BE PERFECT, BUT EMPOWER ME TO BE THE BEST DAD I CAN BE FROM THIS DAY FORWARD.

DAY 2

ONE OF A KIND

*Yes, the body has many different
parts, not just one part.*
1 CORINTHIANS 12:14 NLT

Each child is unique. Even children raised by the same parents in the same home are often radically different. We dads discover this in many different ways.

For example, a dad was reading his young daughter the children's storybook *Frosty the Snowman*. Things were going along fine until they got to the part where Frosty melts. Then the tears started flowing. *Frosty melted!* "It's okay," her dad said. "Frosty will come back." But that didn't comfort her. For days she mourned the loss of this magical snowman. Nothing her dad could say or do would stem her grief. *Frosty melted!* She was inconsolable.

Clearly this was a dangerous story to share with children, and the father tried to protect his second child, a son, from hearing it. But word leaked out, and the boy exhibited an entirely different reaction: He looked around the room at nothing in particular. "What?" he said. "Someone melted?"

The third child held up his imaginary flamethrower and smiled. "I bet I could get him to melt a lot faster." The fourth child, another daughter, expressed her thoughts like this: "Serves him right. If he's dumb enough to go dancing around on a warm, sunny day, he deserves to melt!"

No wonder as fathers we find that each child presents unique challenges and opportunities. What works with one child may not work with another. We love all our children equally, of course, but the relationship we have with each is unique.

Likewise, God honors the singularity of each of His children. No cookie-cutter formula works for a relationship with God, because each of His children is one of a kind. We need not fret if our relationship with God doesn't look like someone else's. He relates to each of us as individuals.

FATHER IN HEAVEN, THANK YOU FOR SEEING ME AS A UNIQUE INDIVIDUAL AND FOR LETTING ME KNOW THAT I WILL NEVER BE JUST A FACE IN THE CROWD TO YOU.

THE POWER OF WORDS

"Bless me—me too, my father!"
GENESIS 27:34 NIV

Suppose humans had the power to make something happen just by speaking it. How would we use that power? What would we bring into being? It's easy to imagine all sorts of good things, from ending world hunger to conjuring up an enjoyable family vacation.

In fact, our words *are* powerful, especially in the lives of our children. For example, our words give our children a sense of identity. "You are designed to make a difference. You are beautiful. You are capable." The way we see and define ourselves is critical. It's the foundation our future is built on. If our children believe they have what it takes, they will move through life with confidence and assurance. If they believe they are loved and lovely, they won't feel the need to seek love and affirmation in the wrong ways.

With our words, we help our children imagine a brighter future. We inspire them to go after higher goals and more meaningful achievements by saying things like, "I can see you bringing much good into your world. You have a heart to care for the needy. You have a sharp mind to help other people solve difficult problems."

In ancient cultures, the father pronounced a blessing over each of his children. This blessing was a pivotal event in a child's life. We continue this practice, not so much with a onetime event, but with the words we use every day. Those words, pregnant with purpose, will give birth to a ripple effect that will touch future generations.

Unfortunately, some of us missed out on this blessing from our own earthly father. And yet God provides. Drink deeply from the affirmation that our heavenly Father gives us. With it comes the power to bless the children He has given us.

FATHER IN HEAVEN, SHOW ME WHAT YOU THINK AND FEEL ABOUT ME. EMPOWER ME TO USE MY WORDS TO BLESS MY CHILDREN. LET THAT BLESSING BRING MUCH GOOD INTO THEIR LIVES.

DAY 4

PRAY, PRAY,
AND PRAY AGAIN

*"Keep on asking, and you will receive what you ask for.
Keep on seeking, and you will find. Keep on knocking,
and the door will be opened to you. For everyone
who asks, receives. Everyone who seeks, finds. And
to everyone who knocks, the door will be opened."*
MATTHEW 7:7–8 NLT

Some guys develop a philosophy of life early on. Others find
that it hits them—like the proverbial ton of bricks—after
much hard experience. One guy in his forties, crawling
out from under the rubble, stated his as, "God gave me
kids to make me pray."

All Christian men know that prayer is good, helpful,
and expected. And most of us do pray—giving thanks over
meals, asking for wisdom on the job, imploring God to help
our friends who are going through hard times.

But there's something about parenting that brings out
the heavy-caliber prayer guns. Maybe your kids are easy

and don't require that kind of prayer. But most of us will have moments—or days or weeks or years—of desperate, frightening, no-other-option-but-God life circumstances that demand *prayer*.

And not just a quick "Please bless my kids, Lord." It will be the kind of prayer that Jesus described in Matthew 7, the prayer that keeps on asking, keeps on seeking, keeps on knocking. This type of prayer is hard work, and there are times when you'll wonder if it's even worth the effort.

But then, at some point, you see the result. Maybe big, maybe small, maybe just the start of a change. . .but an answer. You realize that God is fulfilling Jesus' promise in verse 8: "For everyone who asks, receives. Everyone who seeks, finds. And to everyone who knocks, the door will be opened." But the promise is fulfilled only if we do the persistent praying.

What concerns do you have with your kids right now? Pray, pray, and pray again.

I'M ASKING RIGHT NOW, LORD, FOR
YOUR WISDOM AND STRENGTH TO
BE THE BEST FATHER I CAN BE.
I'M SEEKING AND KNOCKING,
ANTICIPATING YOUR ANSWERS.

THE GIFT OF PEACE

"Peace I leave with you; my peace I give you."
JOHN 14:27 NIV

Even before they can talk, children are attuned to the emotional vibes of the family. They can sense that things are settled and happy or in a state of tension and chaos. Fathers lead the way in this regard. If a father is happy, the family tends to be happy. If he is at peace, he gives his children the priceless gift of peace. But a dad's tension and anger produce unrest.

We all have experienced times when we were not at peace. Stress in the workplace, tensions in marriage, health problems, financial trouble—all of these conspire to rob us of tranquility. In addition, unresolved issues from the past—like geologic fault lines in our souls—threaten our composure when something comes along to trigger us.

How do we find peace in an imperfect world? It starts when we make a practice of lifting every stressful experience up to God and asking Him for His perspective on it. As our heavenly Father, He conveys His peace to us so that we can bring it home to our families.

It's like this: a tiny canoe in the middle of the ocean is thrown around by every little wave, but a huge aircraft carrier slices through stormy seas with ease; the turbulence barely registers. In the same way, as we grow in Christ, our peace grows. The things that previously set us off no longer bother us. We're able to respond to crying babies, grouchy kids, surly teens, and burned toast with equanimity and good cheer.

It's all part of the great adventure. We've found the secret. The power of God's perspective sets us free to be at peace.

FATHER IN HEAVEN, PLEASE SHOW ME HOW TO GET YOUR PERSPECTIVE ON THE THINGS THAT STRESS ME OUT. GIVE ME THE COURAGE TO LOOK HONESTLY AT MYSELF, AND GRANT ME THE GRACE TO RECEIVE FROM YOU THE PEACE THAT IS BEYOND ALL UNDERSTANDING.

THE TRUTH ABOUT FAILURE

We who are strong have an obligation
to bear with the failings of the weak.
Romans 15:1 esv

During a major construction project, there was a mix-up: a manager ordered a crew to pour concrete before the necessary inspections had been made. By the time the manager discovered his mistake, the concrete was rock hard. Jackhammers would be needed to remove it. His mistake would cost his company more than a million dollars and jeopardize the production schedule for the entire project. With much fear, he went to the office of the CEO and reported what he had done. *I'm finished*, he told himself. *Not only will I get fired, but no construction company will ever hire me again.*

The CEO listened to the man's entire report, along with his apology. After a long silence, he said, "People who never make mistakes never get anything done." The meeting was over. The manager kept his job and went on to have a long and successful career.

Making mistakes is part of the human experience. Our children will fail. They won't win every football game. They may bring home an F on a report card. The police may show up at the door. A teenage daughter may break the news that she's pregnant.

Our children's mistakes—large or small—provide us with opportunities to fortify our children with the truth: "You got an F on a report card, not an F in life." "You made a bad decision. We've all made bad decisions. We learn from them, and we grow." "This setback does not define you. I am with you. We will tackle this thing together."

In short, we treat our children as our Father in heaven treats us. We are not defined by our mistakes but rather by God's redemptive love.

GOD, THANK YOU FOR LOVING ME IN SPITE OF MY FAILURES. THANK YOU FOR USING MY MISTAKES AS AN OPPORTUNITY TO MOLD ME INTO A BETTER PERSON. EMPOWER ME TO ENCOURAGE MY CHILDREN WHEN THEY STUMBLE. MAY THEY NEVER BE DEFINED BY THEIR MISTAKES.

THE LANGUAGE OF LOVE

Love (God's love in us) does not insist on its own rights or its own way, for it is not self-seeking.
1 CORINTHIANS 13:5 AMPC

One father was trying to build a relationship with his young son, who didn't want to be hugged, didn't like to talk, and showed little interest in sports. Gifts meant nothing to him. One day, soon after the family moved to a new town, the dad took his son for a walk. Few words were spoken as they walked to the edge of town, sat down in a field, and watched the clouds go by. After a while, they stood up and walked home. Later, the boy said to his dad, "That was the best time I ever had."

We all experience love in our own way. Words of validation that one child drinks up may mean nothing to another child. A daughter may treasure forever a gift carefully selected for her, while a son in the same family might ask himself, *Why is my dad trying to buy my love? Why won't he just spend time with me?* Some children thrive on wrestling and hugs, kisses and pillow fights.

Others tune in when we take time to help with a school project. Some kids love to joke and laugh, while others feel disrespected by the same behavior. Some love to hug, and some want no one, including Dad, in their personal space. Some daughters love to go on a daddy date, while others would rather not. The language of love varies from person to person. As dads, we must learn to translate our love into the words and actions that will mean the most to each of our children.

God Himself recognizes our language of love and speaks it fluently. As we love our children as individuals, we pave the way for them to experience the love of God.

HEAVENLY FATHER, THANK YOU FOR ALLOWING ME TO EXPERIENCE YOUR LOVE. PLEASE TEACH ME MY CHILDREN'S LANGUAGE OF LOVE SO THAT THEY MAY FEEL DEEPLY LOVED BOTH BY ME AND BY YOU.

HUMBLING EXPERIENCES

*For by the grace given me I say to every one
of you: Do not think of yourself more highly
than you ought, but rather think of yourself
with sober judgment, in accordance with the
faith God has distributed to each of you.*
ROMANS 12:3 NIV

Do you ever feel chagrin when you think of the younger
you? Not that geeky middle schooler who was silly, loud,
and occasionally smelly. But the adult you, in your twenties
or maybe even your thirties, who just didn't understand
life the way you do now?

A man's maturation process hits warp speed when he
becomes a father. BC (before children), life was easy and
fun. AD (after delivery), everything changes. Many guys
realize they knew a lot more about parenting before they
had kids.

But perhaps that was part of God's plan all along.

The Lord hates human pride. The warning He gave His
disobedient Israelites some four thousand years ago is still

a red flag to us: "I will break down your stubborn pride and make the sky above you like iron and the ground beneath you like bronze" (Leviticus 26:19 NIV). Sometimes today, He uses our own kids in that breaking-down process.

Have you noticed how children don't always follow the logical path? What you expect, what the experts describe, what the laws of nature would seem to dictate often just melts away like an ice cube on hot asphalt. These are the times we as dads realize we don't know everything, we don't have all the answers, we don't hold the world together all by ourselves. But there is someone who does—and He's just waiting for you to ask for help.

Humbling experiences can be very good things. In fact, God knows they're sometimes just what a dad needs.

LORD GOD, IT'S HARD TO ADMIT THAT I NEED HELP—BUT I DO, ESPECIALLY IN PARENTING! GUIDE ME IN YOUR WAY TO BENEFIT THE KIDS YOU'VE PLACED IN MY CARE.

CULTIVATOR OF DREAMS

His father wondered what the dreams meant.
GENESIS 37:11 NLT

"What do you see?" a man asked his young son.

"A stick," the son replied.

The man smiled as he pierced the soil with the stick and drove it into the ground in the backyard. "I see a willow tree," he said.

The next day, the boy ran outside. Nothing had changed. The stick was still just a stick. Soon, the boy forgot all about the branch his father had planted; but, over time, the branch took root, and a new tree formed. By the time the boy was a young man, the willow tree towered over him, dominating the backyard.

Some people see sticks; God sees trees. He sees what could be, and He puts a vision for a better tomorrow into the hearts of His children. God puts a snapshot of the future into the minds of our children in the form of dreams, goals, and plans.

As dads, we have the privilege of cultivating those

dreams. We understand that even a strong oak tree starts as a flimsy sapling, so we nurture our children's dreams when they are still delicate and fragile. We encourage our children and imagine possibilities with them. We resist the temptation to force them to be something or someone they are not. We teach them to persevere, to dig deep and reach high, to build a proper foundation and achieve what no one else will ever accomplish.

When we cultivate a child's dreams, we set into motion a series of events that will change the course of many lives. As we release our children to achieve their dreams, we stand back and smile. God is at work. He is creating a better tomorrow for the people He loves.

FATHER IN HEAVEN, THANK YOU FOR PLANTING GOOD DREAMS IN THE HEART OF MY CHILD. GIVE ME THE ABILITY TO CULTIVATE THOSE DREAMS SO THAT MY CHILD WILL BE EMPOWERED TO DO THE GOOD WORK YOU INTEND.

THERE ALL ALONG

*Every good and perfect gift is from above,
coming down from the Father of the heavenly lights,
who does not change like shifting shadows.*
JAMES 1:17 NIV

The experiences we have raising our children can teach us important spiritual principles. For example, one dad shared this story: "When my children were young, they loved candy, like most kids do. We knew that a little bit of candy was okay, but too much wasn't good for their health and for everybody's sanity. This presented a problem. Sometimes the kids had reached their sugar limit for the day about the same time my own sweet tooth kicked in. My wife and I didn't eat candy, but we wanted dessert. However, if we served ourselves a treat, our children would feel that they deserved one as well. We discovered a way around this problem. If we cut our ice cream into rectangular shapes and ate it from a plate with a knife and fork, our children never realized what we were doing. We were simply doing irrelevant adult things. Here we were, sitting at the same table, and they had no idea what they were missing. That didn't last forever, of course. One day, they caught on. 'Hey, you guys have ice cream!' "

Sometimes the best things in life are right in front of us. They can remain hidden, not because they aren't there but because our eyes haven't been trained to see them. For example, most of us know that God loves us unconditionally. But one day God brings that into focus for us, and we begin to see His love everywhere—in the sunrise, in the eyes of our children, in the quiet movement of God's Spirit deep in our hearts. Once we see what God has placed right in front of us, our world will never again look the same.

FATHER IN HEAVEN, OPEN MY EYES. EMPOWER ME TO SEE THE GOOD GIFTS YOU HAVE PLACED RIGHT IN FRONT OF ME. I THANK YOU FOR THE BEAUTIFUL GIFT OF LIFE.

MONSTERS IN THE CLOSET

"Never will I leave you; never will I forsake you."
HEBREWS 13:5 NIV

Most dads know this territory well: leaving a hall light on or checking the closet and under the bed to assure a frightened child that no monsters are lurking about. Most children go through a stage when they are afraid of things that simply aren't there. But we go through the motions because we understand that no amount of reasoning will dissuade a child whose world is inhabited by these imaginary things. Many times our children require reassurance rather than logic.

That's the case with adults sometimes as well. Our world is also inhabited by monsters—those hidden in the closets of our souls. No, they aren't big, green, hairy creatures with lots of legs and distorted faces. They take the form of guilt we can't seem to erase, feelings of incompetence, fears, and isolation. They stem from traumas and tangled-up events from the past, from put-downs that still echo in our minds. We may struggle to forgive ourselves.

We may mask our pain with anger or addiction. Logically speaking, we know that our monsters are just illusions, but that logic doesn't help us any more than it helps our children. We too need reassurance.

The transformation we need comes from inviting Jesus into the closets of our souls to confront the monsters we fear. Only He can give us the power to forgive ourselves, to know who we really are and what we're really capable of, to let go of fear and know that He is always there. As men, we are called upon to slay dragons—our own dragons. But we're not asked to do it alone. This is something that Jesus does with us. All it requires is the courage to open that closet door with Him.

JESUS, I OPEN THE DOOR OF MY SOUL TO YOU. THANK YOU FOR BEING HERE WITH ME WHEN I'M CONFRONTED WITH THINGS I'M AFRAID TO FACE ALONE. SHOW ME WHAT'S REAL; PROTECT ME WITH YOUR REASSURING TRUTH.

DAY 12

JUST ENOUGH, JUST IN TIME

He said, "Jesus, remember me when you come into your kingdom. Jesus answered him, "Truly I tell you, today you will be with me in paradise."

LUKE 23:42–43 NIV

Maybe this passage from Luke seems like a strange choice for a dad's devotional: Jesus' interaction with a convicted criminal as both were dying on crosses? Shouldn't a dad's book be fun and upbeat and encouraging?

Well, as Ecclesiastes tells us, there is a time for everything.

Much of parenting is upbeat and fun. There are happy and memorable days that may extend into weeks and years. We thank God for those good times.

But we live in a broken world, and that inevitably affects our homes. Whether our kids just become surly, know-it-all teenagers or fall off a cliff into far more serious trouble, we as dads need the strength that only God can provide. And He sends His persevering power in response to our prayers.

There are biblical examples of incredible, quick, lavish answers to prayer, and we've seen or heard of such miracles in modern life too. But have you ever noticed how God often delays His answers to the last minute? How He sometimes provides just enough for the need at hand, and no more?

God isn't being apathetic or cheap. He's just building our trust muscles. He's showing us that when we can't fix a hard situation, He has things totally in hand. And He will provide just enough, just in time, so that we can't give ourselves the credit.

That thief on the cross began as a mocker. Then he saw how Jesus responded to the injustice and pain of the crucifixion. When he turned to Jesus in true humility, he got just what he needed, just in time.

If we as dads follow that example, so will we.

HEAVENLY FATHER, IT'S HARD TO WAIT. IT'S FRIGHTENING TO LIVE ON THE EDGE. BUT I KNOW THAT YOU SEE FAR BEYOND MY VIEW. HELP ME TO TRUST IN YOUR PERFECT PROVISION.

MAKING REPAIRS

Jesus went around doing good.
Acts 10:38 nlt

Headlines scream bad news. Tragedy strikes close to home. No one can live long on this planet without coming face-to-face with reality: our world is broken. Things are not as they should be. But into this messed-up world, God arrives with tools in hand to make repairs. We see it in the life of Jesus. No matter what challenge was thrown at Him—hunger, disease, hatred, hurt, or sin—He found a way to fix it. He even repaired the damage done by death when He rose from the grave. When He ascended, He promised to return to set everything right. Meanwhile, God is still in the repair business. He still rebuilds the things that are damaged in our world.

How does He do this? He invites us to join Him. We are His agents, using the influence we have to fix things that are broken, to heal the hurting, while bringing justice, mercy, and good into our world. Every time we mend something that is in disrepair, we are an object lesson to our children. The world is not as it could be, but we join Jesus in making things right. Of course, fixing comes in many forms. Sometimes it means patching a bicycle tire. Sometimes it means holding a sobbing child. It may mean rebuilding an engine or restoring a relationship.

When we invest in the lives of our children by setting things right, we reveal a pattern for them to follow throughout their lives. It may take time and effort and skill, but broken things can be fixed. When we take the time to make things right, we do more than give our children a virus-free computer or a toy train that chugs along a track. We give them hope.

FATHER IN HEAVEN, THANK YOU FOR INVITING ME TO JOIN YOU AS YOU MAKE THINGS RIGHT IN THIS BROKEN WORLD. PLEASE EMPOWER ME TO BRING HOPE AND ENCOURAGEMENT TO MY CHILDREN BY FIXING THOSE THINGS THAT NEED REPAIR.

A WELL-PLACED SHOT

"And lead us not into temptation,
but deliver us from the evil one."
MATTHEW 6:13 NIV

The German battleship *Bismarck* was the largest battleship in the world in its time. It was nearly three football fields long. The weight of water it displaced was about the same as twenty-five thousand automobiles. It carried eight fifteen-inch guns. These guns could fire a one-ton shell that could travel more than eighteen miles at over 750 mph. Not only powerful but accurate, the ship's targeting system aimed those shells so precisely that the *Bismarck* destroyed the British battle cruiser HMS *Hood*, the pride of the Royal Navy. The resulting explosion was recorded as one of the largest explosions in World War II. In addition, the *Bismarck* was heavily armored, so even a direct hit by a torpedo would do little damage. This monster ship was the undisputed heavyweight champion of the seas at the beginning of World War II.

Enter Lieutenant Commander John Moffat, a pilot with

the British Royal Navy Fleet Air Arm. Flying a flimsy Fairey Swordfish biplane, he skimmed the waves in the dead of night, in a David-and-Goliath attempt to take on this behemoth. At exactly the right moment, he released a torpedo, which exploded next to the *Bismarck*'s port rudder, locking the rudder in position and making the ship impossible to maneuver. Although the disabled ship remained dangerous, the Royal Navy was able to surround it and finish it off. In May 1941, the *Bismarck* went to the bottom of the ocean, where it remained undisturbed until the wreck was discovered in June 1989 by the same oceanographer responsible for finding the *Titanic*.

Like the *Bismarck*, men and families are sometimes crippled by a well-placed shot. Even the strongest man has vulnerabilities, and a wise dad knows his weaknesses, understands where he can be tempted, and makes provision against it.

GOD, KEEP ME AWAY FROM TEMPTATIONS THAT COULD HARM ME OR MY FAMILY. PROTECT ME BY YOUR POWER. LET ME PUT MY CONFIDENCE NOT IN MY OWN STRENGTH BUT IN YOU. THANK YOU.

CHANGING DIAPERS

If we confess our sins to him, he is faithful and just to forgive us our sins and to cleanse us from all wickedness.

1 JOHN 1:9 NLT

We all stumble from time to time. We make mistakes. We take the easy way out. We sin. This is something we all have in common. What matters most is what we do after we stumble. Some go into denial, refusing to face their own fallibility. Others use anger as a smoke screen, blaming everyone else for their own failings. Some hide behind an addiction. But it takes courage to look in the mirror and honestly face both the man and the mess.

"I was wrong. I'm sorry." Those are incredibly difficult words for many of us, but they are necessary words. They pave the way for our wrongs to be righted, for our sins to be forgiven, for our relationships to be restored. Facing God and our fellow human beings with a confession and an apology is a necessary step in our journey. Life cannot move forward unless and until we take that step of courage.

What makes confession so difficult? Why do so many men avoid it at all costs? It would seem we secretly believe that a failure invalidates us as human beings. Perhaps we expect to be measured by our mistakes rather than honored for our honesty.

One way to look at this is to think about diapers. Most dads have changed many, many diapers. But when we look into the eyes of our children, we don't think about the diapers we've changed. We never even give that a second thought, because our children mean so much to us. In the same way, when we've sinned, God needs to deal with our sin and do what needs to be done so that we can be clean again. But when He looks at us, He never thinks about our mistakes. Instead, He sees the sons He loves.

GOD, GIVE ME THE COURAGE TO BE STRAIGHT WITH YOU, TO BE HONEST ABOUT MY OWN FAILINGS. OPEN MY EYES TO SEE HOW YOU REALLY SEE ME. FORGIVE MY SINS AND MAKE ME CLEAN.

OBEDIENCE FOR ALL

And when they had brought them, they set them before the council. And the high priest questioned them, saying, "We strictly charged you not to teach in this name, yet here you have filled Jerusalem with your teaching, and you intend to bring this man's blood upon us." But Peter and the apostles answered, "We must obey God rather than men."

ACTS 5:27–29 ESV

Have you noticed that children don't always like authority? As we lay down our fatherly rules, toddlers may throw tantrums. Elementary-age kids might become surly. Teenagers sometimes do both. But are we as dads really much better?

Sure, you may be "the boss" in your home—but that's a delegated authority from the ultimate Boss. And, as Peter and the apostles told the angry Jewish leaders who were trying to shut down this newfangled religion called Christianity, "we must obey God rather than men" . . .even if one of those men is you.

At times, all of us struggle to do exactly what God says. His ways occasionally seem awkward, backward, untoward. We just can't understand why He tells us to do certain things in certain ways. We think He may need our help to come up with a more sensible approach.

But the fact is that we don't have to understand God's ways in order to obey Him. Do our kids always understand (or like) our decision-making? Of course not. And we tell them simply to trust us.

We're older, wiser, more experienced than our kids are. We just know better than they do, and they help themselves by following our guidance.

Now put yourself in the kids' shoes, with God as Father. The previous paragraph applies perfectly, doesn't it? And God tells us just what we tell our kids: "Trust Me. You may not understand, but I have good reasons that are for your benefit. You just need to obey."

When you submit to God's authority, you're setting an example for your kids to follow yours.

LORD, I NEED YOUR HELP TO RESPECT AND OBEY YOUR AUTHORITY, EVERY TIME. STRENGTHEN ME TO SET THAT EXAMPLE FOR MY KIDS.

HONORING IMPERFECT FATHERS

"Honor your father and your mother,
that your days may be long in the land
that the LORD your God is giving you."

 EXODUS 20:12 ESV

In our culture, dads have a less-than-stellar track record. Too many are absent, abusive, or aloof. That means, for many, honoring the father in their lives is a challenge. And yet the Bible commands it. We also know that doing so can set us free from the trap of bitterness, create a culture of respect that we can pass on to future generations, and open the door for us to receive more of the good gifts God has for us. So how do we find the grace to honor a father who made significant mistakes as a parent?

It starts with the realization that our fathers are given to us by God Himself. Sometimes that realization doesn't hit home until the end of a dad's life. As we ponder our relationships with our own fathers, flawed as they may be, a few things come into focus. Dads aren't perfect—many are far from it—but God has used their strengths and their mistakes to mold us into the men He wants us to be. And we too can honor our dads in light of how God has used their inadequate, possibly even hurtful, behaviors to help us become better fathers to our own children.

That doesn't mean we haven't been hurt or that there won't be a need to forgive our earthly fathers. We can't live in denial. We look squarely at the truth. But as we find the grace to release our resentment and give it to God, we create space to see the good that God has brought into our lives through our dads. And in that space, honor will grow.

THANK YOU, GOD, FOR THE DAD YOU GAVE ME. SHOW ME HOW TO HONOR HIM IN A WAY THAT PLEASES YOU. I PRAY THAT A CULTURE OF RESPECT WILL BE PASSED ON TO MY CHILDREN AND TO FUTURE GENERATIONS.

WHEN OUR CHILDREN STUMBLE

*At the proper time we will reap a
harvest if we do not give up.*
GALATIANS 6:9 NIV

Most of us—maybe all of us—expect to raise children who are always obedient, never get into trouble, never get caught in any of the many traps that lay strewn across the landscape of a fallen world. But the reality is that parenting takes place with real people—parents who make mistakes and children who make mistakes.

Real people face real problems. The police show up at the door. The news is not good. Life takes an unexpected detour, and our heads are spinning as we try to keep up, because we never saw it coming.

It's in these moments that our faith can be our greatest ally. God—and only God—can take the threads of a disaster and weave them into something beautiful. He constantly searches for ways to redeem our failures and bring about something good. That's why we never stop believing. That's why we never lose hope. God is still working wonders.

But faith is not just a private affair. Throughout history, God has organized His followers into communities of faith. And for good reason: real men reach out for help. The wisdom and faith of others can help sustain us in our moments of greatest challenge, just as we will help others in their hour of need.

Our faith also teaches us that there is still much good, even in a child who has gone astray. We look for that good. We focus on it. We nurture it. We keep the relationship strong because we know that sowing good into a relationship means that we will reap good back if we don't give up. We persist because we see what others might not see: a better future.

GOD, GRANT ME THE FAITH TO SEE
BEYOND MY PRESENT CIRCUMSTANCES.
ALLOW ME TO SEE YOUR GOOD
PURPOSES ALIVE IN MY LIFE AND
IN MY CHILDREN. OPEN MY EYES
TO SEE THEIR STRENGTHS,
AND GIVE ME THE GRACE TO
KEEP MY RELATIONSHIPS
WITH THEM STRONG.

THE JOURNEY TO FATHERHOOD

Because of the joy awaiting him,
he endured the cross, disregarding its shame.

HEBREWS 12:2 NLT

Most men don't grow up playing house, nor do we start our adult lives imagining ourselves as dads. Our minds might be on college, career, and marriage, but the final step to *family* is a big one. Something needs to change inside us before we are fully prepared for the challenge. One dad describes the change like this: "I remember the moment when I first wanted to be a father. I was taking a walk on a trail out in the country. It was a clear, crisp winter day, and a fresh blanket of snow covered everything. A couple hundred yards away, four young children were sledding down a hill. I suddenly felt a strong urge to join in on the fun, to celebrate life together with them. I knew, of course, that I couldn't. So I just watched them for a minute or two from a distance and then went on with my walk. At that point, I realized something I had never known before. I wanted to be a father."

Among men, the joy of being a dad is a closely guarded secret. Most men don't talk about it; most men don't know *how* to talk about it. But those of us who have made the magical transition from man to daddy are welcomed into an inner circle where we know that fatherhood is much, much more than the sum of soccer games and ballet lessons. Everything about our children gives life a deeper, richer shade of meaning.

That's no surprise when we stop and think about it. Two thousand years ago, Jesus Christ weighed the options and made the tough choice; He chose to die. God gave what was most precious to Him so that He could have what He wanted most: children.

GOD, THANK YOU FOR THE GIFT OF LIFE. THANK YOU FOR DECIDING THAT IT WAS WORTH IT TO HAVE CHILDREN. THANK YOU FOR ALLOWING ME TO BE PART OF YOUR PLAN AND GIVING ME THE PRIVILEGE OF CARING FOR CHILDREN YOU LOVE.

THE PARENTING ROLLER COASTER

A time to be born and a time to die, a time to plant and a time to uproot, a time to kill and a time to heal, a time to tear down and a time to build, a time to weep and a time to laugh, a time to mourn and a time to dance, a time to scatter stones and a time to gather them, a time to embrace and a time to refrain from embracing, a time to search and a time to give up, a time to keep and a time to throw away, a time to tear and a time to mend, a time to be silent and a time to speak, a time to love and a time to hate, a time for war and a time for peace.

ECCLESIASTES 3:2–8 NIV

"Ladies and gentlemen, welcome to the Parenting Roller Coaster. Please keep your feet behind the yellow line as the train enters the station. When the cars come to a complete and final stop, carefully take your seats and buckle in tight. It's going to be quite a ride!"

With a positive pregnancy test or confirmation of an adoption, you're off, climbing that first hill. Bringing your child home is the first of many mountaintop experiences—which, in roller-coaster style, are interspersed with hair-raising plunges into the valleys. The words of Ecclesiastes 3 relate well to our parenting journey.

There's plenty of laughter, and definitely some weeping. As dads, we'll often mend what our kids "tear"—in modern terminology, *break*. We'll learn through painful experience the times to speak up and shut up. We'll always love our children but also hate the world system that seeks to derail them.

It's definitely an up-and-down process. Today, let's commit to working tirelessly toward that time when God makes everything beautiful (Ecclesiastes 3:11). Let's follow Solomon's advice in verse 12: "There is nothing better for people than to be happy and to do good while they live" (NIV).

HEAVENLY FATHER, I THANK YOU FOR THE HIGHS OF PARENTING AND REQUEST YOUR PATIENCE, WISDOM, AND STRENGTH FOR THE LOWS.

STRANGE EXPECTATIONS

"I no longer call you servants, because a servant does not know his master's business. Instead, I have called you friends, for everything that I learned from my Father I have made known to you."

JOHN 15:15 NIV

"If I ever have kids, I'm gonna make 'em behave," a young man said to his friends.

Sometimes we enter the world of fatherhood with strange expectations. In the case of the young man who made this statement, all his thoughts about becoming the police officer of the family went right out the window the first time he picked up his newborn daughter. Almost instantly he realized that being a daddy is much, much bigger than "Pick up your toys," "Take out the trash," "Say please and thank you," and "Be home by curfew."

Is obedience important? Of course it is. But being a daddy is about caring for the heart, soul, and body of a fragile fellow human being. It's about defending, protect-ing, encouraging, helping, inspiring, coaching, nurturing, and providing. "Behaving" is only a small sliver of the pie.

This distinction is important to understand because many people have reduced their relationship with God to bald obedience. *Have I obeyed God today? Am I sinning, or am I righteous?* Yes, it is important to steer clear of lust, gossip, and greed. But God is interested in far more than just managing our behavior. He is the caretaker of our dreams, the guardian of our future, the cheerleader of our present, and the healer of our past. He wants to move beyond a list of dos and don'ts to a rich and meaningful relationship with us.

For some, this is a paradigm shift. It means refocusing on *relationship*, taking time to listen, and sharing our thoughts and feelings with a Father who is so much more than a heavenly policeman. It means opening the door to our world and inviting God to move in.

DEAR FATHER IN HEAVEN, I WANT TO OBEY YOU. BUT I WANT YOU TO HAVE MORE THAN JUST MY OBEDIENCE. I WANT YOU TO HAVE ALL OF ME. I WANT YOU TO FEEL WELCOME AND HONORED IN MY WORLD SO THAT OUR RELATIONSHIP CAN BE ALL THAT YOU WANT IT TO BE.

DAY 22

THINK OUTSIDE THE BOX

*"Now I will tell you new things,
secrets you have not yet heard."*
Isaiah 48:6 NLT

Wojtek was probably the most unusual soldier of World War II. Found in Iran by the Polish Army when he was young and adopted by the soldiers after his mother was killed, Wojtek belonged to the 22nd Artillery Supply Company. He quickly grew, and it wasn't long before he was bigger and stronger than anyone else in the unit. In fact, to demonstrate Wojtek's massive strength, five of the strongest soldiers lined up in a tug-of-war contest against him. With one gentle tug, he pulled all five men to the ground. The soldiers loved Wojtek. He was known throughout the Polish Underground as the "Smiling Warrior."

Wojtek's job was to help carry ammunition to the troops in need. He easily did the work of two or three men. When the unit transferred to Italy aboard a British troop carrier, regulations prevented them from taking Wojtek with them into battle. So the Polish Army did what had never been done before. They drafted Wojtek into the army and gave him the rank of private, even though he was less than four years old. By the way, Wojtek was a Syrian brown bear.

As dads, sometimes we need to think outside the box. Each of our children is unique; the mold was broken the moment each one was made. That means each child needs something a little different from us. What works with one never quite works with another, so no two relationships are the same. We are constantly reinventing ourselves as fathers, adapting to new challenges and opportunities. But that doesn't present a problem, because we are being mentored by a heavenly Father who simply won't fit in a box. His infinite creativity is only a prayer away.

THANK YOU, GOD, FOR SHARING THIS ADVENTURE OF FATHERHOOD WITH ME. THANK YOU THAT YOU HAVE SOMETHING NEW FOR ME EVERY DAY. EMPOWER ME TO THINK OUTSIDE THE BOX SO THAT I CAN BEST CARE FOR YOUR PRECIOUS CHILDREN.

HONOR IS A GIFT

Give to everyone what you owe them. . .if honor, then honor.
ROMANS 13:7 NIV

We want our children to honor their parents, not because we're on some kind of ego trip but because we know this is what is best for them. As children respect their dads, it places them in a better position to benefit from the wisdom that our years of experience bring. Listening makes children teachable, and teachability spares young people a world of pain. We explain to our children that honor is a gift we give to other people. But it's a gift that rebounds to us. When people in authority are dishonored, they may scramble to protect their positions of responsibility, creating an adversarial "us versus them" relationship; but respect disarms this confrontational tone.

By esteeming their parents, children acknowledge that God puts imperfect people in positions of leadership and that someday they too will be placed in a similar position. As we teach our children to respect others, particularly their parents, we set them up to receive God's love and experience a deeper relationship with Him.

The Bible tells the story of a man who was misjudged by his brothers, scorned by his wife, and hunted down like a criminal by his boss. His sons betrayed him, and for much of his life he was a fugitive and a wanted man. How did he respond to all of this? With honor. He showed respect to his boss, and when others wanted to harm that supervisor, he refused to allow it. When his boss came to a violent end, he mourned deeply. Again and again, he honored God and those who frequently didn't "deserve" honor. Where did all of this leave him? He became one of the greatest men who ever lived: King David.

GOD, HELP ME TO CREATE A CULTURE OF RESPECT IN MY HOME. HELP EACH MEMBER OF MY FAMILY TO GIVE YOU THE HONOR YOU DESERVE. SHOW ME HOW TO INSPIRE MY CHILDREN TO ESTEEM THEIR PARENTS AND HONOR ONE ANOTHER.

HOW OLD IS "OLD"?

Train up a child in the way he should go;
even when he is old he will not depart from it.
PROVERBS 22:6 ESV

When you're in your twenties, fifty-year-olds seem ancient. Reach your fifties, and the seventies are younger than you'd ever imagined possible. Clearly, age is a relative thing.

So how old is "old" in Proverbs 22:6?

Some of us have heard this verse taught over the years and take it to mean that good input will automatically yield good output. Then come the terrible twos, the even more terrible teens, or the crazy college years, and we begin to wonder about Proverbs 22:6. Is it an ironclad promise or simply a general observation? Are kids from Christian homes guaranteed to turn out right? And if so, when?

Today's scripture comes from the Old Testament, where we find some rather discouraging stories of godly prophets and kings with rotten kids. On the other hand, there are occasions when a terrible man turns out a wonderful child—consider King Amon and his son Josiah. God creates and allows circumstances for His own wise purposes, and people respond to Him both positively and negatively. But we can be sure of this: He is "patient toward you, not wishing that any should perish, but that all should reach repentance" (2 Peter 3:9 ESV).

The kids God gave you have the advantage of your Christian training and example. Of course, none of us perform perfectly, but God can use our influence to His good and loving end, whether or not we live to see the results.

Hopefully, your kids followed your faith early, eagerly, and every day since. But even if your children jump the rails, know that God still wants them. And He gave us the parable of the vineyard workers (Matthew 20) and the account of the repentant thief on the cross (Luke 23) to show us that He pursues people to the eleventh hour.

How old is old? Trust that God has that answer.

HEAVENLY FATHER, YOU HAVE PROTECTED ME FROM MY POOR ATTITUDES AND ACTIONS. PLEASE DO THE SAME FOR MY KIDS. MAKE THEM COMPLETELY YOURS.

WHEN "NO" MEANS LOVE

Love does not delight in evil but rejoices with the truth.
1 CORINTHIANS 13:6 NIV

Some years ago, a group of school administrators noticed that kids at school gathered at the fence separating the school property from the rest of the world. The administrators didn't feel it was healthy behavior, so they tried an experiment. They removed the fence. The effect was different than what they predicted. The kids seemed lost. They milled around in small groups close to the school building. The fence, social scientists concluded, provided security. Once the fence was gone, the feeling of security went with it.

As dads, we put up "fences" for our kids. We need to place boundaries on their behavior for their own safety and well-being. Being a dad sometimes requires us to take an unpopular stand with our children. We can't always say yes. We may need to say no to that extra piece of candy, or we may need to tell a teen that the party that "everybody" is going to is off-limits. Navigating through those tough conversations is never easy. Our children may not understand why we are refusing to grant them the permission they desire. But we have a responsibility for our children, and we sometimes need to draw the line and say no. It comes with the territory.

"No" is also part of God's vocabulary. It isn't the only word He uses. He loves to say yes. But when we experience a *no* from God, how can we perceive that refusal as an act of love? We start with honesty. We tell Him how the *no* feels and why it makes us feel the way it does. Then we listen and learn. Maybe the *no* is just a stepping stone to a much bigger and better *yes*.

GOD, I WANT TO SHARE WITH YOU WHAT I EXPERIENCE WHEN YOU SAY NO. THANK YOU THAT "NO" IS PART OF YOUR VOCABULARY OF LOVE. EMPOWER ME TO UNDERSTAND YOUR HEART TOWARD ME.

DAY 26

PREPARING FOR ANY EMERGENCY

Let all the faithful pray to you while you may be found; surely the rising of the mighty waters will not reach them.

PSALM 32:6 NIV

Preparation is everything. We don't wait until the house is engulfed in flames before we go out and buy a fire extinguisher. We don't wait for the tornado to strike before we determine the safest place of shelter.

People who train military personnel and police officers understand that people in a crisis situation will respond as they've been conditioned to respond. The truth of this was made clear years ago when a police officer was shot in the middle of a gunfight because he was frantically looking around for a can in which to place his empty shell casings. After that, law enforcement training agencies reevaluated their approach and made their training more realistic. Likewise, martial artists practice the same technique over and over again so that if they ever need to use it in real life, their response is automatic. It's called "muscle memory." They don't need to think about it; they just do it.

How do we prepare spiritually for those moments when our world is turned upside down? We understand that God is our first and last line of defense in any kind of crisis. We need the spiritual muscle memory of turning to God in times of need. This is one reason why we put certain spiritual rhythms in our lives. We make a practice of nourishing our souls with God's words from the Bible. We make a habit of taking our needs and the needs of our families to God in prayer. We know that an enduring relationship with God is far more than a "foxhole faith." When we are secure in our relationship with God, we never go through a crisis alone.

GOD, I DON'T KNOW WHAT THE FUTURE MIGHT BRING, BUT I DO KNOW THAT I DON'T WANT TO FACE IT WITHOUT YOU. PLEASE KEEP ME CLOSE TO YOU, AND CARRY MY FAMILY THROUGH ANY CRISIS WE MAY EXPERIENCE.

HOME FROM JAIL

"Celebrate and be glad, because this brother of yours was dead and is alive again; he was lost and is found."
LUKE 15:32 NIV

It was Christmas morning. As the pastor prepared for the service, he felt excited about sharing his holiday message with his congregation. He was wearing his most festive suit and smiling as he headed out. His son had left a few minutes earlier, and the pastor looked forward to meeting up with him at the church. But as he drove over the crest of a hill, a scene unfolded before him that he never expected. His son's car was pulled over, surrounded by four police cars. His boy was in handcuffs, and the police were searching his car.

The pastor went to church that Christmas morning, but his son went to jail. The pastor preached his sermon as planned, never saying a word to anyone about what had happened. Later, his son called from jail, asking his father to bail him out, but the pastor refused. He was seething with anger. These thoughts kept going through his mind:

We've given you everything. We sacrificed for you, and you threw it all away!

Even after a friend bailed the son out of jail, the pastor's anger continued to fester, so much so that he couldn't even look at his son. He fully expected that his wife would share his anger, but that's where he ran into something unexpected. When their son walked in the door, his wife threw her arms around him. "Welcome home, son," she said. In that moment, the pastor understood—for the first time—God's unconditional love for us.

People think of God as the man in the sky who is so angry with us that He doesn't even want to look at us. But that's not His heart. Instead, His arms are open, and He's waiting for the opportunity to say, "Welcome home, son. Welcome home."

THANK YOU, GOD, FOR YOUR WELCOMING LOVE FOR ME. PLEASE OPEN MY EYES TO SEE MY CHILDREN THROUGH YOUR EYES. LET MY CHILDREN LEARN UNCONDITIONAL LOVE FROM ME BY THE POWER OF YOUR GRACE.

TRUE LOVE

"Greater love has no one than this:
to lay down one's life for one's friends."
JOHN 15:13 NIV

It's no exaggeration to say that a good dad would take a bullet for his kids. He would jump in front of a speeding car to shove his child to safety. He would hand over the final life jacket or parachute. This is a picture of the true, selfless, agape love of Jesus that propelled Him to the cross.

Of course, such selfless love should also characterize our marriages—the apostle Paul taught that men should love their wives "just as Christ loved the church and gave himself up for her" (Ephesians 5:25 NIV). But there's just something about our kids—in their youth and naivete, in their need for protection and guidance—that compels dads to cheerfully make great sacrifices. True love does such things.

You will give up lots of time and energy for your children. You'll part with immense quantities of money. You'll lose sleep, skip meals, even lend out your beloved car when they start driving. But more than anything else, you'll devote yourself to heavy-duty prayer for their spiritual well-being. True love does these things too.

It's nice to give your kids gifts, but physical things can't compare with your time, your attention, your energy, and your example. No man parents perfectly, but every dad is divinely appointed to the job of raising the children God gave him. True love calls you to reach beyond yourself, to give more than you think you can, to admit your failures and make them right. True love means you'll lay down your life—maybe literally, certainly figuratively—for your kids.

This is all possible due to the true love God shows you in Christ. "We love because he first loved us" (1 John 4:19 NIV). Love so that your kids will ultimately say the same of you.

HEAVENLY FATHER, GUIDE ME INTO YOUR TRUE LOVE. HELP ME PAST MY SELFISHNESS TO LOVE MY CHILD THE WAY YOU HAVE LOVED ME.

UNEXPECTED HELP

I look up to the mountains—does my help come from there? My help comes from the LORD, who made heaven and earth!
PSALM 121:1–2 NLT

Life is full of surprises. For Sara Tucholsky, the unexpected happened three times in one day.

Sara played softball for Western Oregon University. At five feet two inches tall, she was anything but a heavy hitter. Line drives were her specialty. She had never hit a home run in her life. But one day in 2008, while playing against Central Washington, a miracle happened, and the ball sailed over the fence. With both teams fighting for the conference championship, these three RBIs mattered. As Sara started to run around the bases, in her excitement she forgot to tag first base. Realizing her mistake, she whirled around—and that's when the unthinkable happened. Her knee blew out, and she dropped to the ground in excruciating pain. Slowly, she crawled back to first base, where she remained, unable to move.

What to do? The umpires ruled that if she didn't complete the run around the bases, her home run would be reduced to a two-run single. If her teammates helped her, she would be called out.

That's when Mallory Holtman, Central Washington's first baseman and career home run leader, stepped forward with an idea. After a hasty conference with the umpire, Mallory's plan was approved. Moments later, she and one of her teammates, Liz Wallace, gently lifted Sara and carried her around the bases, pausing at each one to allow Sara to tag it with her uninjured foot. Only about a hundred people were at the game to witness this stunning act of kindness, but word quickly spread, and for the next several weeks it made headlines all over the nation.

This act of kindness reminds us of the kind of God we serve. When parenting and life bring us to the end of our resources, God—in ways we would never expect—carries us home.

FATHER, THANK YOU FOR SEEING AND KNOWING THE LIMITS OF WHAT WE CAN DO. THANK YOU FOR NOT LEAVING US STRANDED WHEN WE FALL. THANK YOU FOR CARRYING US HOME.

NEVER GIVE UP

Love never gives up, never loses faith, is always hopeful, and endures through every circumstance.
1 CORINTHIANS 13:7 NLT

"I was a great parent until I had kids." The man who said this reflects what we all know to be true: there are no perfect dads. Parenting happens in real time with real people. In the mix of the moment, mistakes are made.

Let's face it: sometimes we're clueless. Children don't come with an owner's manual, and every child presents unique challenges. We're figuring it out on the fly. The ship of parenting is built mostly at sea.

This is where a mixture of humility and hardheaded stubbornness serves us well. We need enough humility to recognize when we've made a mistake, to apologize, to make things right. But we also need enough tough-minded determination to get back in the game, even when we get knocked down. Parenting isn't easy. But we don't bail. We stay in for the long haul, even when we feel like throwing in the towel.

Winston Churchill became one of the towering figures of the twentieth century because he recognized the threat of Nazi aggression long before it was the popular view. Later, when England stood alone against the most powerful military coalition of that day, Churchill dug in his heels and declared, "Never give in—never, never, never, never, in nothing great or small, large or petty, never give in. . . . Never yield to force; never yield to the apparently overwhelming might of the enemy."

We persevere because that's what Jesus did for us. He didn't feel like going to the cross, but He did it anyway. He showed us the way when He put aside His comfort and safety and stepped out in front of the train of humanity's hatred to take the hit for us.

GOD, EMPOWER ME TO PERSEVERE. I WANT TO BE THE BEST DAD I CAN BE, BUT I KNOW I'M HUMAN. I KNOW I'LL MAKE MISTAKES. THAT'S WHY I NEED YOU TO PICK ME UP WHEN I FALL AND GIVE ME THE DETERMINATION TO GET BACK IN THE GAME TO WIN.

WHEN GOD SPEAKS

*You have taught children and infants
to tell of your strength, silencing your
enemies and all who oppose you.*

PSALM 8:2 NLT

One day, in northern India, a group of militants gathered around a Christian school, shouting accusations and threats. The leader of the school stepped outside to calm the crowd, but his efforts backfired when the mob dragged him into their midst and started beating him. He was the father of a baby girl. This child was old enough to walk but could only speak a word or two. In the confusion that followed, she somehow slipped away from her caretaker and wandered out to the crowd to see what was happening to her father.

Just in time, one of the women from the school saw her. This little girl was in terrible danger. So the woman ran outside, swooped up the baby, and dashed to the women's dormitory. She got inside and locked the door just ahead of the furious mob.

Enraged, the persecutors tried to break down the door. When that didn't work, they doused the building with kerosene and tried to set it on fire, while the women inside screamed in understandable hysteria.

In the midst of this chaos, the frightened women heard a tiny voice. It was the little girl. She said, " 'Why are you so afraid? Don't you know that you are the apple of My eye?' " In that moment, the scene inside was transformed. Terror gave way to peace. Screaming changed to songs of praise. After several unsuccessful attempts to burn the building down, the crowd dispersed.

How do we hear the voice of God? We hear it in unexpected places at unexpected times. If we're listening carefully, we sooner or later hear it in the words of our children. When that happens, time stands still, and we know we are in the presence of God.

DEAR GOD, OPEN MY EARS TO HEAR YOUR VOICE. LET ME RECOGNIZE WHAT YOU ARE TEACHING ME THROUGH THE CHILDREN YOU HAVE GIVEN ME. THANK YOU FOR BEING PRESENT IN MY FAMILY.

PERFECT FOR THE JOB

Moses said to the LORD, "Pardon your servant, LORD. I have never been eloquent, neither in the past nor since you have spoken to your servant. I am slow of speech and tongue." . . . Moses said, "Pardon your servant, Lord. Please send someone else."

EXODUS 4:10, 13 NIV

A used-car dealership used this tagline to advertise its vehicles: "They may not be perfect, but they may be perfect for you."

Maybe we as Christian dads should claim that concept for ourselves.

Fatherhood provides innumerable opportunities for joy and satisfaction, the feeling of a day well spent and a job well done. But it also offers plenty of pitfalls, moments when we might say or do things we regret. What guy hasn't looked back on his parenting and wished he'd done better?

Though perfection is the believer's goal (see Matthew 5:48), nobody achieves it in this life. That's why God the Father sent His Son, Jesus—to live and die flawlessly, then apply His perfection to those who humbly request it.

God knows you're going to fail sometimes. That's why we have scriptures like 1 John 1:9. But even though you're not perfect, you're the "perfect" guy to parent your kids. You're the exact man God gave them. His choices and reasons are far beyond our understanding, but know this: God never makes mistakes.

Think of Moses. One of the greatest figures of all human history doubted his own ability to lead the Israelites out of their slavery in Egypt. But God had hand-selected Moses for the job, and the Lord would see him through to success. God will do the same for us as Christian dads, as long as we're willing to let Him lead.

No, you're not perfect. But you're the perfect dad for your kids. Thank God for trusting you with the job. . .and get to work.

LORD GOD, GUIDE ME BY YOUR GRACE IN THE FATHERING ROLE YOU'VE GIVEN ME. MAY I NEVER WASTE TIME WORRYING OVER MY SHORTCOMINGS, SINCE YOU ARE READY AND WILLING TO OVERCOME THEM.

CROSSING THE FINISH LINE

*My only aim is to finish the race and complete
the task the Lord Jesus has given me.*
ACTS 20:24 NIV

Runner Derek Redmond was one of Britain's stars in the four-hundred-meter dash. Twice he had set a new British record in the event. Despite numerous injuries and eight surgeries, he had come back to win a world championship and was now poised to win big at the 1992 Summer Olympic Games in Barcelona, Spain.

Two hundred and twenty-five meters into the semifinals, Redmond's hopes for a gold medal were dashed when a new injury to his left hamstring forced him to his knees. Alone on the track with sixty-five thousand people in the stands and millions watching by television, Redmond struggled to his feet with one goal in mind: to get to the finish line.

So much of life is about finishing. As fathers, one of the biggest gifts we can give our children is to finish well and teach them to do the same.

Apparently, Derek's father, Jim Redmond, had the same idea. Waving aside the security guards around the track, Jim jumped over the rail and ran toward Derek. "That's my son," he yelled, "and I'm going to help him."

Derek Redmond didn't win a medal that day, but that moment has been celebrated as one of the most memorable moments in Olympic history.

Like Derek Redmond, we started out well. But then we stumbled. The race we wanted to win, we lost. Our Father in heaven could have stayed in the stands and let us fight it out on our own. But He didn't. Instead, God clothed Himself with human flesh, jumped the rail, and joined us on the track. Together we will cross the finish line.

LORD, THANK YOU FOR NOT STAYING IN THE STANDS. THANK YOU FOR NOT LEAVING ME INJURED AND ALONE ON THE TRACK. I INVITE YOU INTO MY LIFE. LET'S FINISH THIS RACE TOGETHER.

REFUELING SELF-ESTEEM

To all who did receive him, to those who believed in his name, he gave the right to become children of God.
JOHN 1:12 NIV

With high-powered impact wrenches driven by compressed nitrogen, a NASCAR pit crew can change all four tires in less than twenty seconds. Their whole mission is to get their driver back on the track as quickly and safely as possible.

Sometimes being a dad is like being on a NASCAR pit crew. Our job is to get our children back into the race. With statements like "You are capable," "You are beautiful," "You can do it," and "I believe in you," we refuel their self-esteem and strengthen our kids for the road ahead.

Some people worry that complimenting children will swell their pride, transfer their confidence from God to self, and rob them of needed humility. In practice, however, the opposite is true. Insecurity often drives pride and false humility. Children with healthy self-esteem know their place in the world. They aren't easily discouraged or deterred from achieving their God-given purpose. Children with strong self-esteem know they're loved, capable, and lovely. This makes them much less susceptible to negative peer pressure, life-controlling issues, exploitation, and manipulation. It's a tough world out there, but we can equip our kids to be tough enough to thrive in it if we teach them who they really are.

Children, even the ones who seem to be ignoring us, are constantly looking to their dads for affirmation. One father started signing all his letters and emails to his adult daughter with "I'm proud of you." That simple change has transformed their relationship.

When we build our children's self-esteem, we emulate what God has done for us. The Bible is clear. We are created to live forever, designed to make a difference. We carry God's presence into the world. We are the triumphant sons of God.

GOD, EMPOWER ME TO TELL MY CHILDREN THE TRUTH ABOUT WHO THEY REALLY ARE SO THAT THEY MAY CARRY YOUR PRESENCE INTO THE WORLD WITH CONFIDENCE AND DETERMINATION. THANK YOU.

75

OVERCOMING HARDSHIPS

*Endure hardship as discipline; God is treating
you as his children. For what children
are not disciplined by their father?*
HEBREWS 12:7 NIV

On the morning of June 6, 1944, 156,000 Allied troops fought their way onto the beaches of Normandy, France. The scene was a mixture of horror and chaos as the carefully laid plans of Operation Overlord met with bad weather, human error, and the relentless resistance of a determined military foe. Even though there were no safe places, each soldier, sailor, airman, and marine pressed on, drawing on every ounce of courage they could muster. After enormous sacrifice and countless acts of bravery, these troops secured a foothold on the Continent, pushed back the occupying army of Nazi Germany, and liberated Europe from Hitler's domination.

While we admire the heroism of our forefathers, we are also sobered because we never know what kinds of challenges a new generation will face. How do we prepare our children for an uncertain future?

Part of that preparation involves giving our children a chance to work their way through tough situations. Age-appropriate challenges present our children with opportunities to learn and grow strong. The story is told of a young boy who observed a butterfly just beginning to emerge from its cocoon. Seeing how the creature was struggling to get free, the boy thought to help the butterfly by cutting the cocoon open. The result? The butterfly emerged with a swollen body and shriveled wings. Robbed of the opportunity to struggle, the butterfly was unable to force the fluid from its body into its wings. It remained like that—crawling around, unable to fly—until it finally died.

In our own faith journeys, we often take our biggest steps forward as a result of trials. They strengthen us for whatever the future may hold. The opportunity to struggle and overcome—that is a gift from God.

THANK YOU, GOD, FOR THE OPPORTUNITY TO STRUGGLE AND OVERCOME. THANK YOU FOR TEACHING US THE VALUE OF DEPENDING ON YOU WHEN TIMES ARE BAD AS WELL AS GOOD.

FAITHFUL FATHER

*Being confident of this, that he who began
a good work in you will carry it on to
completion until the day of Christ Jesus.*
PHILIPPIANS 1:6 NIV

Looking back over the years, as he watched his boys mature into successful adulthood, a man in his midfifties marveled at God's faithfulness. In spite of great upheavals in his home—including a job loss, an interstate move, and a messy divorce—this man's boys were following Jesus, marrying Christian girls, and starting their own families. The dad fought back tears while telling his story.

God's nature is to be faithful. All of the promises He makes have been, are being, or will be fulfilled—even if we ourselves are unaware of the good He's doing.

It seems reasonable to believe that the more faithful we are to God, the smoother our kids' path will be. And yet we all know of good men with troubled children, and troubled men whose kids rise above the bad example they witnessed. Whatever we may do, positive or negative, God

Himself is always faithful—and He longs for every human being to be part of His family through faith in Jesus Christ (see 2 Peter 3:9).

Sadly, many people resist God's generous offer of the forgiveness of sin. Many will live dark lives that block out the light of Christ. At least they try.

But God is *still* faithful to pursue people—including our wayward kids—in hopes of drawing them into His forever home. If they refuse, the burden is not on Him. If they accept—and we pray that this group includes all of our children—the praise goes entirely to God.

When the Lord saved you, He began a good work that He's promised to see through to completion. When He gave you your children, He was making their path to heaven that much easier. Your job is to live faithfully, love lavishly, and pray, pray, pray for those kids. Then trust that God is a faithful Father who wants their well-being even more than you do.

FATHER IN HEAVEN, I KNOW YOU LOVE MY KIDS DEARLY. PLEASE MAKE UP FOR MY FAILURES WITH YOUR FAITHFULNESS AND DRAW MY KIDS INTO YOUR FOREVER FAMILY.

GETTING OUR CHANCE

*Let us not become weary in doing good, for at the
proper time we will reap a harvest if we do not give up.*
<small>GALATIANS 6:9 NIV</small>

As dads, we know that everyone deserves a chance to take
a shot and make a difference. At age two, Jason McElwain
was diagnosed as autistic. As a high school student, he
desperately wanted to be a basketball player. But between
his five-foot six-inch stature and his autism, the only
role he could find on the team was that of manager. At age
seventeen, he ran the clock, kept statistics, and carried
water bottles to the players. But he did this with such
enthusiasm that the coach decided to reward him with
some time on the court. He just needed to find the right
moment.

That moment came when the team was playing an old
rival. With four and a half minutes left in the game, Jason's
team was up by twenty points. It seemed safe to let him
play, so the coach pointed to him and said the words that

Jason had waited his entire high school career to hear: "You're in."

He got the ball early, took a shot and missed. He tried again and failed. You could feel the tension in the crowd. On the sidelines, people were silently praying, *Please, God, let him make a shot.* Then, with three minutes and twelve seconds left on the clock, something magical happened. The ball traveled from Jason's hands, arced through the air, and—*swish!*—dropped through the basket. Everyone was on their feet cheering. But it didn't stop there. Now that he was dialed in, Jason made shot after shot. When the final buzzer sounded, he had scored twenty points for his team.

The God we serve deeply understands our need for a few minutes on the court. He hasn't forgotten. We each will get a chance to make a difference.

THANK YOU, GOD, THAT YOU GIVE EVERYONE A CHANCE TO PLAY IN THE GAME OF LIFE. THANK YOU FOR THOSE MOMENTS YOU GIVE MY CHILDREN—AND ME—ON THE COURT. EMPOWER ME TO USE MY TIME FOR YOUR GLORY. AMEN.

FINDING TIME

There is a time for everything.
ECCLESIASTES 3:1 NIV

How do kids spell love? T-I-M-E. Many children measure how much they are valued and cared for by the minutes and hours that moms and dads give them undivided attention. One successful father said, "I used to get upset when my neighbor's kids made such a big deal over their dad coming home from work. Why didn't my kids celebrate my arrival? One day, I realized the answer. My neighbor's kids were starved for their dad's attention. My own children got a healthy dose of it every day."

How do we do it? The responsibilities of everyday life can easily fill twenty-four hours a day before we even factor in one or more children. How do we create time for our kids?

It helps to embrace interruptions. Kids live in the now. They have no idea that we're on a schedule. They just know that, in this moment, either we care enough to listen or we don't. When we study the life of Jesus, we discover that most of His greatest moments were interruptions—Zacchaeus, Bartimaeus, Jairus, the calming of the sea—all of these and many more recorded events were departures from His itinerary. But He didn't seem to mind. In fact, it seemed that Jesus thrived on interruptions, having the ability to see the potential of each new opportunity.

It may not be convenient, but our children need our undivided attention. That means setting aside the phone, turning off the television, putting down the book, and actively listening. We may not always be able to give our children the time they desire, but each moment we share with them is both a gift and an investment. It reminds them and us that we have a Father in heaven who always has time for us.

GOD, GRANT ME THE ABILITY TO UNDERSTAND WHAT'S IMPORTANT IN THE NOW. HELP ME TO SHIFT MY FOCUS TO MY CHILDREN WHEN THEY NEED MY ATTENTION. ENABLE ME TO GIVE THEM THE GIFT OF TIME.

NEVER STOP GROWING

*The hearts of the wise make their mouths prudent,
and their lips promote instruction. Gracious words are a
honeycomb, sweet to the soul and healing to the bones.*

PROVERBS 16:23–24 NIV

The fruit doesn't fall far from the tree. Our children become what we are. We lead—positively or negatively—by our example far more than we do by our words or instructions. Modeling attitudes and behaviors for the next generation is one of the greatest gifts we can give. So, how do we become someone we would want our children to emulate?

One of the best ways to guide our children is by exemplifying teachability. Openness to instruction is important because it sets the stage for growth throughout life. The person who has stopped learning has stopped growing. In the classic Aesop fable "The Tortoise and the Hare," the tortoise wins the race because he keeps on going when the hare stops to nap. In similar fashion, the teachable person keeps on growing, even when others stop. When we are teachable, we hold the belief that every person and every circumstance has the power to teach us something. . .if we're willing to learn. A teachable man shows an active eagerness to improve, a lifelong quest to discover, and an ability to accept and evaluate criticism without getting defensive.

Teachability should not be confused with passivity or an inability to lead. We still pilot the ship even when we're looking for ways to improve. In the Bible, King David's sons were his royal advisers. He listened to their input so that he could do his job of leading even better.

Sometimes it's difficult to learn, particularly from someone who doesn't treat us with respect. But if we're willing to listen, God is always willing to give us His perspective on other people and trying circumstances. Life's greatest lessons can come from the most unexpected places.

GOD, PLEASE OPEN MY MIND AND MY HEART TO LEARN FROM OTHER PEOPLE AND TO RECOGNIZE THE LESSONS YOU HAVE PLANTED ALL AROUND ME. LET ME PASS THE QUALITY OF TEACHABILITY ON TO MY CHILDREN.

TIME FLIES

Teach us to number our days,
that we may gain a heart of wisdom.
PSALM 90:12 NIV

"Time flies when you're having fun," they say. But time also flies when fun is in short supply. Time simply flies.

We may not sense the passage of time at every moment. But one day you wake up and realize a lot of proverbial water has flowed under the bridge. You begin to understand the biblical sentiments like

> *Our days may come to seventy years,*
> *or eighty, if our strength endures. . .*
> *they quickly pass, and we fly away.*
> PSALM 90:10 NIV

> *"My days are swifter than a weaver's shuttle. . . .*
> *My days are swifter than a runner."*
> JOB 7:6; 9:25 NIV

There are moments when realizations of this sort really hit dads. It seems like you've just brought a baby home, and then you're sending him off to kindergarten. . .or summer camp. . .or the senior prom. The busyness of the baby and toddler years may distract you from the speed of time's passage. But around their fifth-grade year, the afterburners kick in. In the blink of an eye, they're graduating. . .getting married. . .having kids of their own.

Certainly, we raise our kids for this very purpose. We teach and train them, we prepare them for their own adult independence. But it can be shocking how quickly that time arrives.

And that's why Moses' prayer in Psalm 90:12 should be regularly on our lips. We have a limited amount of time to ready our kids for life, and we need to take full advantage of every moment God gives us. Time—and wisdom and strength and mercy and goodness—are never limited with Him. So consciously ask for the help and provision He's happy to offer.

The time will come when time is no more. And all the hard work we put into our children will be rewarded forever. Teach us, Lord, and give us a heart of wisdom.

LORD GOD, GRANT ME AN UNDERSTANDING OF LIFE'S BREVITY—AND THE WISDOM AND STRENGTH I NEED TO GUIDE MY CHILDREN TOWARD YOU.

BUILDING OUR HOME

"I am going away to prepare a place for you."
JOHN 14:2 AMPC

A construction contractor called a crew leader into his office. "I'm putting you in charge of building a home," he said. "As with all our jobs, quality matters. This is important to me, and I'm trusting you to do the job right. Use the best materials, and use the best practices."

Unfortunately, the crew leader was less than trustworthy. He built the home, but he cut corners everywhere. Instead of insisting on excellence, he settled for mediocrity. After a few months, the job was done, and he reported back to his boss.

"Are you satisfied that you did your very best?" the owner of the company asked.

"Yes, sir," the crew leader replied.

"Good," the boss smiled as he handed him the keys, "because this is now your home. I had it built for you."

As dads, we are constantly building our own homes. We're not building with two-by-fours, drywall, and siding, but rather with words, leadership, and acts of kindness. We understand this. We care. We want our homes to be as close to heaven as possible for our children.

It seems fitting that Jesus spent his young adult years as a carpenter. He knows how to build things that last. He has gone ahead of us to build a home for us in heaven. And that home is not mainly about streets of gold or mansions in glory. It's about each of us feeling at home, where everyone will care and be cared about, where every person will experience the presence and love of God.

Jesus invites us to join His construction crew. We have a hand in building that eternal home by how we value and care for those God puts in our path. . .starting with our children.

JESUS, THANK YOU FOR BUILDING AN ETERNAL HOME FOR US. PLEASE EMPOWER ME TO BUILD A STRONG HOME FOR MY CHILDREN WHERE THEY WILL FEEL LOVED AND CARED FOR.

WRONG DIRECTION!

*"Come to me, all you who are weary and
burdened, and I will give you rest."*
MATTHEW 11:28 NIV

On the evening of Tuesday, September 6, 2011, a train departed from Tirupati, India, with more than one thousand passengers aboard. The next morning, the train arrived 850 miles from its intended destination after traveling in the wrong direction. An investigation revealed that a railroad employee had entered the wrong code, placing the train on the wrong track. Other railroad employees were literally sleeping on the job, so no one noticed the mistake until the next morning. Passengers and officials were both grateful and relieved that the train didn't collide with another train during the thirteen-hour journey away from its expected stop.

As dads, one of our biggest jobs is teaching our children to take the right track and travel in the right direction. Although numerous safeguards exist to keep trains, planes, and automobiles from going the wrong way, we humans are afflicted with damage to our internal navigation system. For us, it can be counterintuitive to travel in the right direction.

For example, when we stumble (as we all do), our natural tendency is to hide from God—just as Adam and Eve hid from God in the garden after eating the forbidden fruit. We hope to clean ourselves up so that God won't be disappointed with us. But that never works. We don't have the ability to clean up or dress up for God. Only God can make us clean.

This is why it's so important that we be thoughtful about how to respond to our children's mistakes and misbehavior. If our children see that our focus is on restoring them, then they can approach God with confidence. Instead of avoiding God, they can go to Him for restoration—and so can we.

FATHER IN HEAVEN, PLEASE HELP ME TO COME TO YOU WHEN I LEAST FEEL LIKE IT—AND ESPECIALLY WHEN I WANT TO AVOID YOU. EMPOWER ME TO TEACH MY CHILDREN TO DO THE SAME.

TEACHING INTEGRITY

The power of the wicked will be broken,
but the LORD upholds the righteous.
PSALM 37:17 NIV

Two maple trees stood in the family's backyard. They were about the same height, about the same age. In fact, on the outside, they looked alike in almost every respect. But there was a difference. One night, a violent storm swept across the state. The winds were high, a tornado warning was issued, and the family huddled in the basement. When the storm passed, their home was fine, but the backyard was not. One of their two maple trees had fallen, split right down the middle. In the light of the next day, it became clear why one tree stood up to the storm and the other did not. The heart of the fallen maple was rotted, which compromised the strength of the tree. The damaged tree was unhealthy on the inside.

On the outside, people too can look much alike. We don't get to see what's in their hearts. Sometimes it takes the storms of life to bring to the surface what is really there.

We build character in our kids, knowing that integrity is the best form of self-defense. We can overcome seemingly insurmountable obstacles if we are clear that our cause is just. What is integrity? It's the ability to keep a promise, even when it hurts. It's doing what's right when no one but God is watching. It's not taking the easy way out. Integrity empowers us to stand alone when everyone else wants to do wrong. It's standing for the truth, whether it's in style or not. It's a refusal to be bought and a determination never to compromise with evil.

If our children grow up with a strong moral compass, they can filter through many options and choose the high road. It becomes a way of life for them.

GOD, PLEASE ENABLE ME TO MODEL AND TEACH INTEGRITY TO MY CHILDREN. WHERE I HAVE FALLEN, EMPOWER ME TO MAKE THINGS RIGHT, AND GIVE US ALL GRACE TO LEARN FROM OUR MISTAKES.

ZIP THE LIP

Saul's anger flared up at Jonathan and he said to him, "You son of a perverse and rebellious woman! Don't I know that you have sided with the son of Jesse to your own shame and to the shame of the mother who bore you?"

1 SAMUEL 20:30 NIV

Quick, easy takeaway from this scripture: never, *ever* talk to your kids like this.

God's Word pulls no punches. It always shows us the true condition of humanity—the sinful, selfish, scathing side of our personalities. And a scene like this one, featuring the increasingly unhinged King Saul and his son Jonathan, is a jarring reminder for us as dads to control our tongues.

Saul faced a lot of pressures, but there's simply no excuse for words like these. . .ever. Can you imagine the pain they must have caused Jonathan? And he was a truly noble young man.

Hopefully, your kids are Jonathanesque. But they are

only kids, and they will occasionally try your patience. There are times when their level of respect might leave something to be desired. But however old they are, they're always younger and less mature than *you*. And you, Dad, have the obligation to respond to their poor behavior in an exemplary way.

Jesus never lashed out at His persecutors. He sometimes spoke the truth quite firmly, but it was always in love, as the apostle Paul later taught (Ephesians 4:15). Many times, we'll all do better to follow Solomon's advice, and say very little: "The one who has knowledge uses words with restraint, and whoever has understanding is even-tempered. Even fools are thought wise if they keep silent, and discerning if they hold their tongues" (Proverbs 17:27–28 NIV).

Think back to your own childhood. Were you perfectly respectful and obedient? Would you (or did you) enjoy being treated as Jonathan was by his father?

Right now, before the heat of the moment, say a prayer. Ask God to calm and control your reaction when the kids start pushing your buttons. Ask Him to help you zip the lip.

**LORD, PLEASE SPEAK
YOUR LOVE THROUGH ME,
EACH AND EVERY TIME.**

SOURCE OF CONFIDENCE

"How can you believe since you accept glory from one another but do not seek the glory that comes from the only God?"
JOHN 5:44 NIV

Some people feel as if they need to have a certain title on their business card, a certain car in their driveway, a certain number on their paycheck in order to feel okay about themselves. Others receive validation from trophies celebrating past accomplishments or the praise of friends and coworkers. Some look for affirmation in more destructive ways, through extramarital affairs or life-controlling addictions. Some tally up their good deeds or their religious activities.

Most people know that these external "measuring sticks" provide a fragile foundation for confidence and self-esteem. Money and prestige can be gone in an instant. Our past—good or bad—doesn't define us. We can never be good enough. Self-destructive choices haunt us instead of helping us.

Construction contractors build high by digging deep. The higher the building, the more important the foundation. Likewise, confidence—that magical something that carries us through life's ups and downs—must rest on something solid. Our faith in God's ability to use us for good, and our own sense of being okay, depend on this foundation.

As dads, we want our children's confidence grounded in something strong enough to stand up to life's storms. But how do we establish a stable foundation? The path to confidence, ironically, travels straight through our insecurities. Every time we feel unsettled or off-balance and we bring our secret fears to God, it's an opportunity for Him to tell us the truth about who we are, who He is, and how He feels about us. His perspective empowers us to live life on His terms, with overwhelming confidence in His power to carry us through.

GOD, WHEN MY CHILDREN ARE INSECURE AND AFRAID, EMPOWER US AS A FAMILY TO GET YOUR PERSPECTIVE. I PRAY THAT MY KIDS CAN GO THROUGH LIFE FILLED WITH CONFIDENCE BASED ON YOUR TRUTH.

REJOICING WITH OTHERS

Be happy with those who are happy.
ROMANS 12:15 NLT

One of the greatest gifts we can give our children is freedom from jealousy. Envy destroys relationships, breaks up families, and can be the driving force behind all kinds of evil. In the Bible, resentment caused the young men in one family to sell their brother into slavery.

What drives this ill will? It comes from a mindset of scarcity. In the Soviet gulag, prisoners sometimes murdered one another over a scrap of bread that most of us would refuse to eat. In the same way, brothers and sisters sometimes squabble, competing for what they think is a limited supply of parental love and approval.

Let's look at this from the other side. Imagine the world's wealthiest man. Would it upset him that his neighbor got a new car or that his best friend received a promotion at work? Not likely!

When things aren't going our way and others around us are receiving praise, gifts, and rewards, how do we find it in our hearts to rejoice with them over their success? We need God to show us all over again how wealthy we are in Him. As sons of God, we are members of the wealthiest family in the universe. There is no limit to what our Father in heaven will give us in His wisdom and in His timing.

This is why we lavish our own children with love. We want them to know how much they are valued and cared for. We want them to be filled to overflowing with love and acceptance, partly so that they can honestly smile and be glad when good things happen to others in their world. We want to be a conduit through which they can experience God's limitless love.

GOD, LET ME BE A CHANNEL THROUGH WHICH YOU CAN POUR OUT YOUR LOVE ON MY CHILDREN. LET THEM EXPERIENCE THE ABUNDANCE OF YOUR LOVE SO THAT THEY WILL NEVER BE CAUGHT IN THE TRAP OF SMALL—MINDED SCARCITY.

STANDING TOGETHER

"I pray also for those who will believe in me through their message, that all of them may be one, Father, just as you are in me and I am in you."

JOHN 17:20–21 NIV

Two brothers were fighting. Their father separated them, took them out to the backyard, and told them to gather up sticks that had fallen from a recent storm. Taking some twine from the garage, the dad tied the sticks together in a bundle and handed it to his younger son. "Break this," he said. The boy strained to break the bundle but failed. His older brother looked on, confident that he could do better. But when his turn came, he too found it impossible to break the sticks when they were tied together. Pulling out a jackknife, the father cut the string and handed each boy individual sticks from the bundle. "Break these," he said. Apart from the bundle, the sticks broke with ease. "These sticks are like members of a family," the dad explained. "When we stand together, we stand strong. But when we fight, when we are divided, we lose the strength of family.

We become easy targets."

Most of us know this old story—adapted from an Aesop fable. But most of us have little training or experience in building family unity. It's a tall order, particularly when the people living under one roof can be so completely at odds with one another at times.

As men, we lead the way in making family our priority. Many other things compete for our time, but it's hard to imagine anything more important than the people God has entrusted to our care. We model reconciliation, peacemaking, and conflict resolution for our children. We accentuate the strengths of each family member and openly express our appreciation for each person. We do these things because that's what Jesus has done for us. Apart from Him, we would squabble over our many differences. But He died to make us one.

GOD, PLEASE BRING MY FAMILY TOGETHER. EMPOWER ME TO INSPIRE LOYALTY AND UNITY. FORGIVE ME WHEN I AM PART OF THE CONFLICT INSTEAD OF PART OF THE SOLUTION. MAKE US ONE.

THE MIRACLE OF LIFE

This is what God the LORD says—the Creator of the heavens, who stretches them out, who spreads out the earth with all that springs from it, who gives breath to its people, and life to those who walk on it.

ISAIAH 42:5 NIV

New parents thrill to every milestone, big and small, that their baby reaches. From the first smile to the first word, from the first time sleeping through the night to those first unsteady steps, the child is attaining wonders never before witnessed in human history.

At least, that's the way it feels to Mom and Dad. The fact is this: these things have happened literally billions of times before. That reality, though, doesn't diminish the truly amazing nature of the life God has gifted you with. Your child *is* a miracle, something you should always acknowledge with gratitude to the Creator of all good things.

It is God who, as Isaiah 42:5 declares, gives breath and life to all people—all of us who inhabit this earth on which we walk. It is God who directs our steps (Proverbs 20:24), if we—and, we pray, our children—are wise enough to follow Him. It is God who, in His great love and mercy, provides both our physical life on this earth and the opportunity for a new spiritual life that lasts forever.

The children God gives us should draw our thoughts back to these basic truths. This broken world system opposes God at every turn, and we can find ourselves caught up in far lesser things—sometimes sin, often the typical distractions of jobs and bills and entertainments. But in His grace, God sends the miracle of new life to remind us of Himself.

Why not take a moment to acknowledge His goodness, the many blessings He's provided to you and your offspring, who come from His hand. It's all a miracle, you know?

HEAVENLY FATHER, I THANK YOU FOR THE BREATH THAT FILLS ME AND THE FAMILY YOU'VE GIVEN ME. MAY I ALWAYS SEE THIS LIFE YOU'VE CREATED AS MIRACULOUS.

DAY 49

THE TEAM

In Christ we, though many, form one body,
and each member belongs to all the others.
ROMANS 12:5 NIV

Rick Hoyt was born with cerebral palsy. During labor and delivery, the umbilical cord was wrapped around his neck, blocking the flow of oxygen to his brain. It soon became clear that he would be a quadriplegic. Doctors encouraged his parents to place him in an institution, but his parents refused. They were determined to give their son a full and rich life. At age eleven, Rick was given a computer device that enabled him to communicate, allowing him to attend school. He went on to graduate not only from high school but from college with a degree in special education.

Meanwhile, something powerful was unfolding in the life of his family. When Rick was fifteen years old, his father, Dick, decided to enter a five-mile race to benefit an athlete who had been paralyzed in an accident. Even though Dick wasn't a runner, he decided to run—not alone, but with his son. He pushed Rick in a wheelchair. After their first race together, Rick said, "Dad, when I'm running, it feels like I'm not handicapped." Inspired to continue, Dick Hoyt trained incessantly, and the two entered more races. To date, they've competed in more than one thousand endurance events, including seventy marathons and several Ironman competitions. They even ran and biked across the United States. Team Hoyt, as they are called, was inducted into the Ironman Hall of Fame in 2008 and was honored with a bronze statue erected near the starting line of the Boston Marathon.

Without Rick, his dad would be just another runner. And without his dad, Rick would be just a guy with cerebral palsy. But together they have inspired, encouraged, and educated millions of people around the world. They perfectly illustrate what every dad instinctively knows: we need each other.

THANK YOU, GOD, FOR GIVING ME A FAMILY. THANK YOU THAT WE ARE FAR MORE TOGETHER THAN WE EVER WILL BE SEPARATELY. EMPOWER ME TO CONVEY THIS IMPORTANT TRUTH TO MY CHILDREN BY WHAT I SAY AND DO.

GOD'S REPRESENTATIVE

We are therefore Christ's ambassadors,
as though God were making his appeal through us.
2 CORINTHIANS 5:20 NIV

Mahatma Gandhi once said, "If Christians would really live according to the teachings of Christ, as found in the Bible, all of India would be Christian today." No doubt he was thinking of an infamous experience he'd had as a young man in South Africa. After studying law in England, Gandhi worked as an attorney in South Africa. There he became fascinated with the teachings of Jesus and considered becoming a Christian. But his desire to become a Christian came to an abrupt end one day when he decided to visit a local church. A man standing at the door barred him from entering. When he patiently explained that he wanted to worship with that congregation, he was called a derogatory name based on his race and threatened with physical expulsion if he didn't leave voluntarily.

We can argue that this tragic incident is yet another example of imperfect people misrepresenting a perfect

God. From the Spanish Inquisition to the white supremacist movement, much has been said and done in the name of Jesus that has no connection to Him at all. There is wisdom in teaching our children that just because people claim to represent Jesus doesn't mean they actually do.

But there is a more important reminder here for us as dads. We, as parents, are our children's first exposure to God. Everything we say and do models God to our impressionable young children, whether we want it to or not. How our children relate to us will form the foundation of how they relate to God. That's why our job is so important. Unlike the man who barred Gandhi's way into the church, we welcome our children to Jesus. We teach them who He is not just by our words but also by everything we do.

GOD, PLEASE WORK WITH ME SO THAT I CAN HELP MY CHILDREN KNOW WHO YOU REALLY ARE. PLEASE EMPOWER ME TO LEAD MY CHILDREN TO JESUS BY WHAT I SAY AND WHAT I DO.

THE GIFT OF LAUGHTER

*[God] will yet fill your mouth with
laughter and your lips with shouts of joy.*
JOB 8:21 NIV

A large and important part of being a dad is having fun
with our kids. Shared laughter is a precious gift we give
our children. It builds emotional equity in our families,
giving us the relational capital we need when it comes
to lead. Laughter soothes pain, defends against hurt,
and brings families together.

Opportunities for fun are everywhere. Running through
the lawn sprinkler on a hot summer day, pillow fights,
long walks in the woods—creating laughter-filled memories doesn't need to cost anything but time. One dad hid
loose change around the house and invited his children
to keep whatever they found. Another dad divided up
the Lincoln Logs and toy soldiers between his two sons.
When Mom was away, they built forts for their soldiers
and then attacked the enemy fortifications with a bag
of marbles. Exploring a riverbank, building a tree house,

organizing a neighborhood game of football—the possibilities are endless. Sometimes these fun moments can happen spontaneously, like making silly faces in front of a mirror or taking turns creating lines of audio for a muted television commercial.

There are boundaries, of course. We never laugh at someone else's expense. Humor at home is never meant to harm; and if it does, we heal the hurt right away. At the same time, as dads, we don't take ourselves too seriously. We let our children laugh with us. We know that there's a time to be goofy and there's a time to be serious.

Many people view God as deadly serious all the time. But inside the family of God, there is ample room for fun. Heaven will be, among other things, a place of laughter. God invented fun, and He knows how to laugh with us.

GOD, THANK YOU FOR THE GIFT OF FUN. HELP ME TO CREATE MANY HAPPY, FUN-FILLED MEMORIES WITH MY CHILDREN. HELP US AS A FAMILY TO LAUGH TOGETHER. I PRAY THAT MY CHILDREN WILL KNOW YOU AS THE GOD WHO BRINGS LAUGHTER.

ABBA, FATHER

*For those who are led by the Spirit of God are
the children of God. The Spirit you received
does not make you slaves, so that you live in fear
again; rather, the Spirit you received brought
about your adoption to sonship. And by him we
cry, "Abba, Father." The Spirit himself testifies
with our spirit that we are God's children.*

ROMANS 8:14–16 NIV

Few pleasures compare with hearing your little one call
you "daddy." It's a term combining equal parts love and
trust. It's a name that communicates peace and joy. It's
the utterance of an intimate relationship. And it's a joy
for us as fathers.

Somehow, the almighty God who made and fills the
universe gains the same pleasure when His kids call out
to Him. Sure, we respectfully address God as "our heavenly
Father," and that is absolutely proper. But we also have
the right and privilege to talk to God more intimately,
to approach Him like a three-year-old does his "daddy."

God is our *Abba,* an Aramaic term that implies affection, closeness, and trust.

Why can we be so familiar with the awesome Creator God? Because of our faith in His Son, Jesus, who died on the cross to pay the penalty for our sins. Our belief in Him saves us and makes us the dwelling place of the Holy Spirit. As adoptive sons of God, we can now pray just as intimately as Jesus Himself did in the garden of Gethsemane on the night of His arrest: "*Abba,* Father," he said, "everything is possible for you. Take this cup from me. Yet not what I will, but what you will" (Mark 14:36 NIV).

You want your kids to know you, enjoy you, communicate with you, love you. Your heavenly Father desires all of those things too. As soon as you finish this reading, why not give Him a call? Your *Abba,* Father will be thrilled to hear from you.

ABBA, FATHER, I LOVE YOU.
HERE IS WHAT'S ON MY HEART. . . .

LEARNING TO FORGIVE

Forgive as the Lord forgave you.
Colossians 3:13 NIV

Jim and John were going into business together. They each needed five thousand dollars to get the business started, but neither had any money. So they decided to borrow from family. Jim's family was struggling, but they managed to scrape up the money for him to borrow, contingent on his maintaining a strict repayment schedule. John's family had money to spare, and they easily wrote him a check for the full amount.

Unfortunately, the business failed, leaving Jim and John with nothing. They had to go back to their families and break the bad news. "I'm broke. I don't have the ability to repay this loan. I'm sorry. Is there any way you can cancel the debt?"

John's family said, "You tried your best. It didn't work out. Don't worry about it. We don't even miss the money." But Jim's family was in a different place. "We needed that money to pay our bills. Now that you can't repay us, how will we pay the rent or put food on the table?"

As Christians, we are called upon to "cancel the debt"— that is, to forgive those who hurt us. This is one of the most difficult requirements of the Christian life. . .and one of the most difficult lessons to teach our children. Why is it that some people are able to forgive with ease while others struggle to forgive?

The answer has to do with our own spiritual wealth. If we've had a deep encounter with Christ in those places where we've been hurt, if we've been enriched with the certainty of who we really are in God's family, then forgiving others becomes manageable. We measure the hurt of their offense against the magnitude of God's love for us, and smile.

GOD, PLEASE ENABLE ME TO BE A CHANNEL OF YOUR LOVE TO MY CHILDREN SO THAT THEY WILL HAVE THE INNER STRENGTH TO WITHSTAND THE STORMS OF LIFE. WHEN THEY GET HURT, BRING YOUR COMFORT AND REASSURANCE TO THEM. EMPOWER THEM TO FORGIVE.

BREAKING BARRIERS

"The Kingdom of Heaven has been forcefully advancing."
MATTHEW 11:12 NLT

At 215 Montague Street in Brooklyn, New York, a plaque reads, "On August 28, 1945, Jackie Robinson, a rising star of the Negro Leagues, met with Branch Rickey, Dodger president and general manager, and signed an agreement to play in the Dodger organization. This initiated the process of becoming the first African-American player on a major-league baseball team—integrating the major leagues and making baseball truly the pastime of the entire nation."

Even once the agreement had been signed, it didn't come to fruition until April 15, 1947, when Robinson broke the "color barrier" that had prevented African Americans from playing in the major leagues and stepped out to play ball for the Brooklyn Dodgers. From that point forward, he endured taunting, racial slurs, hate mail, and worse. But he never lost his focus. He simply played great baseball.

His dedication paid off. By 1949, the Negro Leagues

were virtually a thing of the past, as all the best players had been recruited into the major leagues. Robinson had proven to his generation what we take for granted today: African Americans could excel at anything, and baseball was no exception. It takes a certain kind of courage and foresight to break barriers and pioneer new territory. One or more of your children might be a Jackie Robinson of tomorrow, proving to their generation that the "impossible" can be done if one simply has the faith and dedication to do it.

This is why we take seriously the dreams of our children. This is why we give them opportunities to persevere through hardship to meet age-appropriate challenges. We are training them to create a better future, just as God is training us to pioneer new territory for Him.

GOD, PLEASE EMPOWER ME TO PREPARE MY CHILDREN FOR THE CHALLENGES THEY WILL FACE. GIVE ME THE FAITH TO BELIEVE THAT YOU CAN DO THE IMPOSSIBLE THROUGH MY CHILDREN, AND LET ME COMMUNICATE THAT CONFIDENCE TO THEM.

DAY 55

RUNNING AWAY

*"You will know the truth, and the
truth will set you free."*
JOHN 8:32 ESV

A woman who had been shopping stepped out of the store and got into her car. As she left the parking lot, she noticed that a large truck was following her closely. She turned left on the next street. The truck turned as well. She sped up. The truck kept up. When she slowed down to allow him to pass, he slowed down and showed no interest in going around her. By now she was becoming concerned. She pulled onto the highway, and the truck followed. When she changed lanes, he changed lanes also. Finally, she took an exit and looked for a convenience store. Pulling into the parking lot, she slammed on the brakes, threw open her car door, and raced into the store to summon help.

The truck driver also stopped, jumped out of his truck, and ran toward the woman's vehicle. But instead of following the woman into the store, he wrestled to the ground the convicted rapist who had been hiding on the floor of her back seat. From his vantage point high up in the cab of his truck, he had been able to see what the woman couldn't. He knew where the real danger lay.

For most people, the things we run from are our own fears, shame, and insecurity. As men, we tend to cover over these feelings with anger or push them away with denial. But we'll never know real peace until we open up those inner fears to Jesus. We must face them in order to be whole. From that place of wholeness, we are then equipped to convey God's love to the next generation.

GOD, GRANT ME THE COURAGE TO FACE
THOSE BROKEN PLACES IN MY SOUL
SO THAT I CAN BE STRENGTHENED
TO CARRY YOUR LOVE TO MY CHILDREN.
THANK YOU FOR WORKING INSIDE
MY HEART AND SOUL TO MAKE ME
A BETTER FATHER.

AS JACOB GREW

As [Rachel] was having great difficulty in childbirth, the midwife said to her, "Don't despair, for you have another son." As she breathed her last—for she was dying—she named her son Ben-Oni. But his father named him Benjamin.

GENESIS 35:17–18 NIV

In an extreme, tragic circumstance, the patriarch Jacob lost his beloved wife Rachel in childbirth. Though he had been specially chosen by God—as grandson of Abraham, Jacob played a vital role in the development of Israel—he was also known for selfishness and dishonesty. But in Genesis 35, we see a glimpse of God working in Jacob's life, as He will in all of us who choose to follow Him.

The beautiful Rachel had captured the self-centered Jacob's heart. He was happy to trade seven years of work for the right to marry her. Those years seemed like just a few days to Jacob—but then Rachel's deceitful father married Jacob off to his older daughter, Leah. Jacob could have his dream girl, Rachel, for another seven years' labor.

This polygamous home had little chance of happiness, and things only declined when Leah had children as Rachel couldn't. Competition led the sisters to offer their servant girls to Jacob in an attempt to produce more children for each. The family dysfunction was growing.

Yet there was even more trouble ahead. God finally allowed Rachel to bear Joseph, Jacob's eleventh son and obvious favorite. But a second pregnancy brought Rachel's life to an end. Her dying words were to name the boy Ben-Oni, "Son of My Sorrow."

But here, undoubtedly by God's strength, Jacob rose to the occasion. In spite of his grief, he overruled Rachel's choice, renaming the child Benjamin, "Son of My Right Hand."

If God could cause a selfish, deceitful man like Jacob to slowly but surely grow in faith, He can certainly do powerful things in us. Whatever your own shortcomings, know that if you have believed in Jesus Christ by faith, you have been chosen just as surely as Jacob was—and you can know that the Lord has powerful plans for your life too.

HEAVENLY FATHER, PLEASE CAUSE ME TO GROW AS JACOB GREW.

THE STRAIGHT PATH

We do this by keeping our eyes on Jesus, the champion who initiates and perfects our faith.
HEBREWS 12:2 NLT

A fresh snow had fallen, and a father decided to go for a walk with his young son. As they hiked along the path, the dad said, "Son, I want to challenge you to a contest." He motioned to a fence about thirty yards away. "See that fence?" he said. "I wonder which one of us can create the straightest line of footprints in the snow from here to the fence. You go first." The boy smiled, relishing the challenge. With great care, he put one foot in front of the other, working diligently to keep the line as straight as possible. After several minutes of concerted effort, he reached the fence and looked back to survey his straight line. To his dismay, the line was not straight at all, but meandering and crooked.

"My turn," the dad said. He strode toward the fence, covering the distance in just a few seconds. The boy was amazed. His dad's path was perfectly straight.

"How did you do it?" he asked.

"Very easy," his father said. "I just picked a post on the fence, and I walked straight to it. I didn't worry about keeping my path straight. Instead, I just kept my eyes on the fence post."

As we teach our sons and daughters to live a good life, there are two ways to approach it. Like the boy, we can focus their attention on their steps, focusing on their actions, trying to keep each step straight. Or, like the dad, we can fix our eyes, our attention, our love, on something else—Jesus. We can inspire our children to love God whole-heartedly. When they do, the path will take care of itself.

GOD, PLEASE ENABLE US AS A FAMILY TO FALL IN LOVE WITH YOU. PLEASE INSPIRE MY CHILDREN TO KNOW AND VALUE YOU FIRST AND FOREMOST SO THAT EVERYTHING ELSE IN THEIR LIVES CAN FALL INTO PLACE.

COOLING OFF

"In your anger do not sin."
EPHESIANS 4:26 NIV

A young father labored long and hard, making a model of an ancient sailing ship. At last, he finished and put his creation proudly on display. But their father's masterpiece was not the focus of attention for his two school-age sons. Instead, they were quarreling. The older boy shoved the younger. Furious, the younger son grabbed the television remote and hurled it at his older sibling. Big brother ducked. Mom walked in just as the projectile scored a direct hit on their father's precious creation, shattering it into a thousand pieces. There was a long pause, followed by blame shifting.

"Enough!" Mom said. "Pick up the pieces. Put them on your father's desk. He will deal with you both when he gets home."

The brothers' argument was long forgotten by the time their dad arrived home, replaced by dread for what he would do. They huddled in their room, waiting, listening. Supper was eaten in silence. The boys poked at their favorite meal of macaroni and cheese as if it was boarding-house gruel. That night and the next day, the boys tiptoed around their dad, but he ignored them. Finally, just before supper, he called them over and said, "When I came home and found that you had destroyed something I had worked so hard to create, I was angry enough to push you or throw something at you. Do you know that?"

"Yes, sir," each boy mumbled.

"But I didn't do that. I gave myself a full day to calm down so that I wouldn't do something to you that I would later regret. Do you think you boys could learn to do the same with each other?" By our actions, we teach our children how to control their anger.

GOD, WHEN I GET ANGRY WITH MY FAMILY, PLEASE EMPOWER ME TO PAUSE, TO COOL DOWN, AND NOT TO RESPOND IN ANGER. PLEASE GIVE ME YOUR PATIENCE AND YOUR SELF-CONTROL IN THOSE VOLATILE MOMENTS.

HONEST TO GOD

I cried aloud to the LORD, and he answered me from his holy hill.
PSALM 3:4 ESV

One of the most important steps in our Christian journey is learning to get real with God. Polite prayers may have their place in polite company, but we don't begin to change and grow in our faith until we start bringing our real thoughts and feelings to God. Do we have doubts? We bring them to God. Do we have fears? We don't deny them; we share them with our Father in heaven. Are we angry? We let God know. Even when we are angry with God—*especially* if we are angry with God—we don't hide our feelings from Him.

We all experience times in our lives when God does not make sense. He may seem far away. He may seem aloof, uncaring, weak, or cruel. In reality, He is none of those things, but we need reassurance, not at an intellectual level but at a deep-down gut level. We sometimes need to get someplace alone and yell out our frustration, our disappointment, our exasperation with God. But then after we've gotten as honest as we know how with Him, we pause. It's His turn to be honest with us. We let Him— by His Spirit, by His Word, by other people—guide us to the truth we need to enable us to get the fresh perspective that turns everything around.

This is why we take time to listen to our children. This is why we don't shut them down when they share honestly from their hearts, even if we don't like what they're saying. We listen. We let them get real with us. And then, after they know that they've been heard, we find that teachable moment and share with our children what they need to know in order to grow.

GOD, PLEASE ENABLE ME TO GET REAL WITH YOU. PLEASE GRANT ME THE GRACE TO ALLOW MY CHILDREN TO BE HONEST WITH ME. GIVE ME THE POWER TO LISTEN, AND HELP ME MAKE THE MOST OF MY TEACHABLE MOMENTS WITH THEM.

GOOD GIFTS

"Which of you, if your son asks for bread, will give him a stone? Or if he asks for a fish, will give him a snake? If you, then, though you are evil, know how to give good gifts to your children, how much more will your Father in heaven give good gifts to those who ask him!"
MATTHEW 7:9–11 NIV

One time, while teaching about prayer, Jesus used an example from fathering. It would be a terrible father indeed who responded to his son's request for bread by handing over a rock. . .or who tossed a writhing serpent onto the plate of a boy who had asked for fish. You don't have to be Father of the Year to meet your kids' basic needs for food—even a bad dad will generally do that.

The lesson for us is that we have a very wealthy, very generous, very kind Father who is eager to meet our needs—and, oftentimes, even our wants. Compared to God, we are evil. . .and yet we love and provide for our children. Won't He be much more generous with us?

Of course He will. And yet the example that Jesus

used raises an important consideration for us as fathers: Aren't you more inclined to give good things to your kids when they're showing you love and respect? Sure, you'll feed them even when their attitude is bad. . .but the special treats might wait until their demeanor improves.

Now put yourself in the kids' shoes. . .because that's exactly where you stand in relation to God. Is your attitude toward Him respectful? Are you obeying Him, cheerfully and consistently? Does your demeanor seem to justify a special treat from your Father?

Yes, God is very gracious, even when we fail. Hopefully, we are gracious when our children misbehave. But the nature of relationships is that respect goes a long way in keeping everyone happy.

Any attitudes you might need to change right now?

MY FATHER, PLEASE FORGIVE ME FOR THE TIMES MY ATTITUDE IS WRONG. HELP ME TO RESPECT YOU AS I SHOULD—AND ALLOW ME TO ENJOY YOUR GENEROSITY.

THINGS TAKE TIME

Rest in the Lord; wait for Him and patiently lean yourself upon Him.
PSALM 37:7 AMPC

It costs more than four billion dollars—that's billion with a *b*—to build a nuclear-powered aircraft carrier. To create this floating fortress that will travel the seas for fifty years with only one stop for refueling, to create four and a half acres of flight deck, to put together a million-plus different parts and nine hundred miles of cable, is a big job. Forty million hours of labor go into its construction. That's the same as one person working nonstop, around the clock, for 4,566 years.

Some things take time. As men, we understand a few things about construction. For example, we know that we can't move into a home on the second day of construction, because there's nothing to move into. At best, there's a hole in the ground and maybe some wet concrete. No matter how patient or impatient we are, the job will still take months to complete.

God understands this reality as well. He understands that it takes time to build a life. Our children don't grow up overnight. They will spend a lot of time doing the silly, immature things that kids do before they leave that season of life behind and move on to a more grown-up way of approaching things.

That's why, as dads, we relax and enjoy the ride. Yes, we are hard at work helping our children construct a good life. Yes, we do our best to build character and teach important lessons. But when our kids act like kids, we smile and accept them for who they are. As we do, we are reminded that our Father in heaven understands that we are works in progress, and He's okay with that. He empowers us to grow, but He doesn't do the entire job overnight.

GOD, PLEASE HELP ME TO BE PATIENT WITH THE PACE OF LIFE. THANK YOU FOR GIVING ME A FRONT-ROW SEAT TO WATCH MY KIDS GROW UP. THANK YOU THAT YOU KEEP WORKING WITH US WITHOUT GIVING UP.

BELIEVE WHAT YOU PRAY

*An angel of the Lord appeared to him, standing at
the right side of the altar of incense. When Zechariah
saw him, he was startled and was gripped with fear.
But the angel said to him: "Do not be afraid, Zechariah;
your prayer has been heard. Your wife Elizabeth
will bear you a son, and you are to call him John."*
LUKE 1:11–13 NIV

A young teen was in a very dark place, and his parents
were struggling right along with him. It seemed that every
aspect of the boy's life was off-kilter, and mom and dad—
and many other relatives and friends—had prayed long
and hard to little obvious effect.

One evening, the husband told his wife of a specific
prayer he had prayed for the boy. Frustrated and irritable,
the wife responded, "That will never happen."

Dad was frustrated and irritable too, but this time,
thankfully, the Spirit shut down any quick reply. He later
approached his wife and gently said, "You know, if we want
God to answer our prayers, we have to believe that He

can and will. Let's not cancel out our prayers with doubt."

The biblical Zechariah learned that his prayers for a son were being answered by the conception of a boy named John. . .who we know as John the Baptist. But Zechariah doubted even the mighty angel that delivered the good news! The man still got his miraculous son, but he was struck mute for nine months as either a punishment or a sign—or both.

May we as fathers never short-circuit our prayers for our kids by assuming God can't or won't answer us. "When you ask, you must believe and not doubt, because the one who doubts is like a wave of the sea, blown and tossed by the wind," a Bible writer said. "That person should not expect to receive anything from the Lord" (James 1:6–7 NIV).

LORD, I WANT YOU TO ANSWER MY PRAYERS FOR MY KIDS. I COMMIT TO BELIEVING THAT YOU CAN AND WILL DIRECT THEIR PATHS.

DAY 63

BRINGING CHILDREN TO JESUS

*"Let the children come to me,
and do not hinder them."*

LUKE 18:16 ESV

About two thousand years ago, there was a man who was going through life as a quadriplegic. Things were extraordinarily hard for him and for those who were taking care of him. But he was fortunate to have good friends. One day, his friends learned that Jesus was visiting nearby. So they put the paralyzed man on a stretcher and carried him on foot to the place where Jesus was. But when they got there, there was no way to get close to Him. The crowd overflowed the house, and people were peering in through the doors and windows.

But then the men came up with an idea. Why not climb onto the roof? It didn't get them all the way to Jesus, but it got them closer. They climbed up onto the flat roof, where another idea occurred to them. Perhaps they could remove the roof tiles and at least see Jesus from above. Once the tiles were out of the way, they decided to go the rest of the way. Tying a rope to each corner of the stretcher, they lowered their disabled companion through the roof right down to the floor in front of Jesus. In a few minutes, the paralyzed man could stand. He could walk. He could jump, dance, and run. He was healed.

So much of being a dad is about bringing our children to Jesus. Yes, there will be obstacles, but we keep finding creative ways around them because connecting our kids with Jesus is everything.

JESUS, MOST OF ALL I WANT MY CHILDREN TO FIND YOU. I WANT THEM TO KNOW YOU, TO INVITE YOU INTO THEIR LIVES AS THEIR LORD AND SAVIOR. SHOW ME HOW TO BRING THEM TO YOU.

YOU ARE THE MAN!

Nathan said to David, "You are the man!"
2 SAMUEL 12:7 NIV

Okay, full disclosure here: what the prophet Nathan said to King David was not at all fun or complimentary. "You are the man!" didn't indicate that David had just made the winning basket or closed an important business deal. It was an accusation—fully supported by the facts—that David had stolen his neighbor's wife. Hopefully, none of us will ever be identified as "the man" in such a way.

But, in a positive sense, "you are the man"—the man God has given to your kids. You are the man called to lead and guide them into the knowledge of Jesus Christ. You are the man expected to protect and provide for them, to teach and to train them in the ways of the Lord. You are the man—so don't ever think anyone else will take care of these duties for you.

When you faithfully perform your God-given tasks, you will see Him work in your kids' lives. Ideally, they'll choose to follow Jesus early and passionately, never straying from the straight and narrow path. Some kids will be slower to come around, and others may jump the spiritual rails for a while. Your kids might not seem to want God in their lives at all—though even their arguing against Him may indicate that He is still, quietly but relentlessly, speaking to their hearts. Whatever the case, you are the man called to love your kids, to pray for them, and to set the example of godliness that will either encourage or convict them regarding their faith.

You are the man to accomplish good things in your kids' lives. Yes, other men—grandfathers, teachers, coaches, neighbors—can play a role too. But the primary responsibility *and privilege* are yours. You are the man—so get to work!

THANK YOU, LORD, FOR GIVING ME THIS AWESOME PRIVILEGE AND RESPONSIBILITY. PLEASE GIVE ME WISDOM AND STRENGTH TO BE "THE MAN" IN MY KIDS' LIVES. I WANT THEM TO KNOW YOU THROUGH MY TEACHING AND EXAMPLE.

TEACHING CHILDREN TO PRAY

*"Lord, teach us to pray, just as
John taught his disciples."*
Luke 11:1 niv

Relationships require communication. In our relationship with God, that communication is called prayer. As fathers, we have the responsibility and the privilege of leading our children into a relationship with God that includes meaningful prayer.

One family did it like this: They kept two jars. When they had a prayer request, they wrote it down and put it in the jar. Later, when the jar was full, they started taking out the pieces of paper with the prayer requests on them. If the request had been answered, they wrote it down in a journal of answered prayers. If the request was still pending, they prayed for it again and put it in the second jar. When the second jar was filled, they repeated the process.

Of course, prayer is much more than just asking God

for things. That's why we incorporate other approaches as well. Another way to teach children to pray is to give them a prayer sentence to complete. For example, "God, today I feel. . ." or "God, the thing I am happiest about is. . ." Some dads use prayer acronyms such as ACTS (A for adoration or praising God, C for confession, T for thanksgiving, and S for supplication—that is, asking God for things). The Lord's Prayer found in Matthew 6 is a model prayer—not just a set of words to repeat but an outline to follow. How do we want to see God's name honored? How do we want His will to be done?

The best way to teach our children to pray is to set an example by practicing meaningful daily prayer ourselves. The more we learn to connect with God, the easier it will be to inspire our children to do the same.

GOD, PLEASE EMPOWER ME TO GUIDE, TEACH, AND INSPIRE MY CHILDREN TO CONNECT WITH YOU IN A MEANINGFUL WAY IN PRAYER. PLEASE BRING YOUR PRESENCE AND YOUR WISDOM INTO THIS PROCESS.

TEACHING THE BIBLE

*You have been taught the holy Scriptures
from childhood, and they have given you the
wisdom to receive the salvation that comes
by trusting in Christ Jesus. All Scripture is
inspired by God and is useful to teach us.*
2 Timothy 3:15–16 nlt

The Bible can have a powerful impact on our children.
A little boy and his dad were having lunch at a hospital
cafeteria on the occasion of the birth of the boy's baby
brother. Evidently, the children's Bible storybook had
made an impression on the little tyke. Taking his cue
from the story of David and Goliath, the youngster stood
up in the booth and turned around and faced the scores
of doctors, nurses, and visitors. Then, at the top of his
lungs, he bellowed out Goliath's challenge: "Choose a
man to fight me!"

We never know what a child might say. But we do know
that the teachings of the Bible have been trusted throughout the ages for spiritual guidance. Unfortunately, many

adults find the Bible a difficult, forbidding book. How can we as dads hope to teach the Bible to our children?

Reading age-appropriate Bible storybooks to our children when they are young can make the job easier. Of course, we don't stop there. As our children grow, we introduce them to portions of the Bible that will be most relevant and helpful. The more at home we are with the Bible, the more we can help our kids. A number of tools are available for this; an online search will show sites and other resources that make the Bible easy to understand. One dad listens to the Bible on his phone as he's falling asleep. He says it helps him understand how the themes and stories in the Bible fit together. Each time we read the Bible with our children, a seed is planted. The harvest is a godly life.

GOD, PLEASE OPEN MY EYES WHEN I READ THE BIBLE TO BETTER UNDERSTAND YOUR MESSAGE. EMPOWER ME TO INSPIRE MY CHILDREN TO READ AND LOVE YOUR WORD. THANK YOU FOR THE WISDOM YOU HAVE SHARED WITH US.

TOMORROW'S LEADERS

*How do you know what your
life will be like tomorrow?*
JAMES 4:14 NLT

When Katie Davis graduated from high school, her parents assured her that she could attend the college of her choice. But a different dream had grabbed her attention. Postponing college for a few months, she climbed onto an airplane, crossed the Atlantic Ocean, and settled into a room in a school in a village in the African nation of Uganda. While her parents waited in Brentwood, Tennessee, things were unfolding for Katie much differently than they had imagined. Homeless children were attracted to this young woman. She somehow found food to feed them, medical care to heal them, and money to educate them. Her room gave way to a house. Little girls who had no place to live moved in with her. One day, the unexpected and miraculous happened. A little girl who had no home, other than the one Katie provided, looked up into her eyes and asked, "May I call you Mommy?" And

Katie found herself saying, "Yes."

Today, Katie is the mother of thirteen adopted daughters. She lives with her family in Uganda. The ministry she started is helping to lift thousands of children out of the grip of poverty. Her story has been told and retold around the world through her bestselling book. Her example is inspiring millions of people to reach out and care for the poorest of the poor.

We never know what kind of beautiful future God has locked up inside the children He has put in our care. God-given passions and desires may take our children to destinations we cannot imagine. Children are the future. As dads, we are coaching tomorrow's leaders.

THANK YOU, GOD, FOR THE PRIVILEGE OF BEING A DAD. THANK YOU FOR THE BEAUTIFUL FUTURE YOU HAVE PLANNED FOR MY CHILDREN. EMPOWER ME TO COACH THEM WELL AND RELEASE THEM INTO YOUR GOOD HANDS.

DISAPPOINTMENT TO CELEBRATION

Jesus continued: "There was a man who had two sons. The younger one said to his father, 'Father, give me my share of the estate.' So he divided his property between them."

Luke 15:11–12 niv

There are moments in our fatherhood journey when we think, *Wait a minute—this isn't what I signed up for!* Perhaps the dad in this parable of Jesus felt that way.

You probably know him as the father of the prodigal son—the man whose younger child basically wished he were dead. What else could it mean when the boy demands, "Give me my share of the estate"?

The story grows sadder as it's told. The father generously fulfills the boy's selfish request. The boy then selfishly blows the money on "wild living" (Luke 15:13 niv). The selfish boy ends up worse off than the pigs he'd been hired to feed, looking longingly at their slop (verse 16).

But then there's a glimmer of hope, a coming to his senses. The son remembers his father—and his father's goodness. "How many of my father's hired servants have food to spare, and here I am starving to death!" he said to himself. "I will set out and go back to my father and say to him: Father, I have sinned against heaven and against you. I am no longer worthy to be called your son; make me like one of your hired servants' " (Luke 15:17–19 niv).

The father couldn't accept those terms. This was his *son*, not a servant! Dad had been watching for the boy all along. When the youngster appeared on the horizon, the father dropped everything and ran to be reunited.

This is the nature of fatherhood. It's how God feels about us and how we feel about our own kids. If (or perhaps when) your child is in the prodigal period, keep watching, keep praying, keep loving. By God's grace, your disappointment may one day turn to celebration.

LORD, CONFLICT WITH MY KIDS IS HARD. GIVE ME YOUR STRENGTH AND LOVE TO PERSEVERE.

DAY 69

FINDING THE NEW

Forgetting what is behind and straining
toward what is ahead, I press on.
Philippians 3:13–14 niv

As dads, we are painfully aware of our imperfections. We wince when we think of moments when we lost our temper, failed to keep a promise, or totally misunderstood one of our children. It's easy to be a great dad in theory, but it's a lot harder in real life.

In real life, children get sick. They don't sleep through the night. They whine. They negotiate. They expect their parents to arbitrate squabbles that would give a television-court judge a headache. They step in front of traffic and go wandering off at the mall. They drag home stray animals. They inform us of commitments they've made about five minutes before the family needs to change course in order to keep them. They come up with the wildest needs at the most inappropriate times. All of this conspires to leave us dads sleep deprived, cranky, clueless, and out of sorts.

Every dad makes mistakes. We fail. We burn out. We wear out. Sometimes we wimp out. We break down. Our patience wears thin. We are imperfect fathers raising our children in an imperfect world. We deeply want to parent well, to care for these precious lives God has put in our hands. But we know that our children are going to grow up with some ugly memories of dad at his worst.

How do we cope with that reality? Beyond the given—apologizing and seeking to make things right whenever we can—we live in the now. Our focus is not on what we did wrong yesterday, but rather on what we can do right today. It's not maintaining a perfect track record that matters. It's finding and doing the right thing right now that counts. We must seize the opportunities as God gives them to us.

GOD, PLEASE OPEN MY EYES TO THE NOW. EMPOWER ME TO SEE WHAT GOOD I CAN DO RIGHT NOW FOR MY CHILDREN. PLEASE FORGIVE MY WRONGS AND UNDO THE DAMAGE I'VE DONE. LET ME BRING GOOD TO MY CHILDREN TODAY.

HEALING OUR WORLD

*Praise be to the God and Father of our Lord Jesus Christ,
the Father of compassion and the God of all comfort.*
2 Corinthians 1:3 niv

We live in a messed-up world, and dysfunctional families are found in every part of it. As dads, we all have moments when we watch other parents bully their children, and we secretly wish we could put that other parent in a time-out chair. (Or maybe we'd like to go a round or two with that dad in the ring!) It is frustrating to watch other people parent poorly. Parental misbehavior can carry a lifelong toll for a child. We all make mistakes, of course, but sometimes the actions of other parents go beyond mistakes. Sometimes it's enough to make us angry. But that anger is all dressed up with no place to go. Outside of those extremely rare occasions when it is necessary to seek legal intervention, there's usually little we can do in the moment to change things. That's tough. No man wants to feel powerless.

But perhaps we're not helpless. Maybe there is something

we can do. Maybe we are growing the antidote for all the venom that is being injected into our world. Among other things, we are raising our children to be healers of the hurt that is felt so deeply by so many. We know that we can all be healers in our own way. Sometimes it's a smile. Or it may be a word of encouragement. Healing might come in the form of friendship or mentoring. Some will raise children who will become professional healers, doctors, nurses, therapists, and counselors. But we all will bring up children who are capable of carrying God's comfort into the lives of hurting people wherever they may be found.

GOD, LET US BE A HEALING FAMILY. EMPOWER EACH OF US TO BRING ENCOURAGEMENT, GOODWILL, AND HOPE TO OTHERS AROUND US. AS A DAD, I WANT TO BE AN EXAMPLE TO MY CHILDREN IN THIS AREA.

DAY 71

A FRESH START

*The kind of sorrow God wants us to experience
leads us away from sin and results in salvation.
There's no regret for that kind of sorrow.*

2 CORINTHIANS 7:10 NLT

A dad decided to take his youngest son sledding. He invited the child's mother to come along, but she refused, rehearsing the dangers of sledding and the seriousness of broken bones. She preferred to worry from the comfort of home. But the dad wasn't worried at all. He dressed his son up in a snowsuit like the kid from the movie *A Christmas Story*. He thought, *What could possibly go wrong?*

The first time down the slope, the sled hit a bump. Boy and sled separated midair, and the boy tumbled down the hill, bouncing and rolling until he finally came to rest at the bottom. Dad watched the whole thing in slow-motion horror, imagining his child unconscious with multiple injuries. The boy lay there for five long seconds as his father made his way down the hill, mentally rehearsing what he was going to say to the 911 dispatcher. But then the child stood up. He looked back up at his dad and smiled. With bright eyes and a cheerful voice, he said one word: "Redo!"

"Redo" has become a motto in that home. When one of the kids rolls his eyes at his mother when she asks him to do something, Dad doesn't say, "Go to your room." He doesn't get angry and launch into a lecture. Instead, he smiles and says, "Redo." This practice helps his kids know that yes, they messed up, but no, it's not the end of the world. They just need to redo.

The reset button for our lives is always available. We all screw up. But we can always turn to God. He is the God of redo, the God of a fresh start.

GOD, I THANK YOU THAT A FRESH START IS ALWAYS ONLY A MOMENT AWAY. AS I RAISE MY CHILDREN, HELP ME TO SHOW THEM THAT WE DON'T NEED TO GET STUCK IN FAILURE, THAT SUCCESS IS JUST A MATTER OF STARTING OVER.

FLOWERY BEDS OF EASE?

"I have told you these things, so that in me you may have peace. In this world you will have trouble. But take heart! I have overcome the world."

JOHN 16:33 NIV

It's sad how many great hymns of the faith have faded from the Christian consciousness. Remember this one?

> *Am I a soldier of the cross*
> *A follow'r of the Lamb?*
> *And shall I fear to own His cause*
> *Or blush to speak His name?*
> *Must I be carried to the skies*
> *On flow'ry beds of ease,*
> *While others fought to win the prize*
> *And sailed through bloody seas?*
> *Are there no foes for me to face?*
> *Must I not stem the flood?*
> *Is this vile world a friend to grace*
> *To help me on to God?*

Sure I must fight if I would reign
Increase my courage, Lord;
I'll bear the toil, endure the pain
Supported by Thy Word.

This hymn by Isaac Watts is just as powerful today as it was when he wrote it in the early 1700s. And while the lyrics aren't about fatherhood, we could easily apply them to our duties.

We're in a war, and we're fighting a very destructive world system on behalf of our kids. There are plenty of foes to face, a flood of evil to be turned away from our homes. We'll need courage from God to bear the toil and endure the pain. Dispense with any notion of "flowery beds of ease."

Let's allow Jesus to conclude this reading: "In this world you will have trouble. But take heart! I have overcome the world."

YES, LORD, I RECOGNIZE THE CHALLENGE OF RAISING KIDS IN A WAR ZONE. GIVE ME WISDOM AND COURAGE TO SEE THEM THROUGH TO VICTORY.

NOW I BELIEVE

Jesus told them, "This is the only work God wants from you: Believe in the one he has sent."

JOHN 6:29 NLT

Becoming a father can be a spiritually transforming experience for us. Every dad's journey is different, of course. One young father had rejected the whole idea of God, possibly because of his experiences with his own father growing up. In that case, his father carried around a laundry list of every time his son had failed. Whenever the dad was angry, he pulled out the list. When it came to the son's failures, the dad seemed to have the memory of an elephant. As he grew older, the boy decided he didn't want any more of that. In his mind, he certainly didn't want or need a God in heaven keeping track of his mistakes and throwing them in his face every chance He got.

But at 3:30 one morning, his wife woke him up. Contractions. And they were getting stronger. They made the drive to the hospital. Hours later, this adrenaline-pumping but exhausting process was coming to a conclusion. Finally, the doctor motioned to the young man. "Dad, do you want to hold your child?" As he held his firstborn son in his arms, it slowly began to sink in: *I am responsible for this life.* He was holding eternity in his hands.

This was the beginning of a whole new dimension in his relationship with God. He began to see that God was not the controlling, angry deity he had imagined. Instead, he saw that God loved him unconditionally just like he loved his new son. And so began his journey to faith.

THANK YOU, GOD, FOR WHAT YOU TEACH US ABOUT YOURSELF THROUGH OUR EXPERIENCE AS DADS. HELP ME TO BE A GOOD DAD TO MY CHILDREN SO THAT THEY CAN SEE YOUR HEART IN MY ACTIONS.

DAY 74

HE IS HERE

God has said, "I will never fail you.
I will never abandon you."
HEBREWS 13:5 NLT

One of the big challenges of faith is trusting a God who appears to be absent for no reason. Many of us have felt abandoned by God during those times when we needed Him most. We don't understand what He is doing or why He seems to delay in coming to our aid.

Parenthood gives us a new perspective on this common issue. As fathers, we know that our children don't always have the same information we have. As a result, their perspective gets skewed; they don't see the whole truth.

A young dad and his son shared a unique connection, a strong father-son bond from the moment the boy was born. One night, the dad put his little baby in the crib to sleep. As soon as he left the room, however, the child started crying. The dad walked back over to the crib. Baby stopped crying. He stepped away; his son cried. He came back; the crying stopped. This happened three or four times. Finally, the dad said to his son, "Even when you can't see me, I'm still taking care of you."

Just as the words left his mouth, something supernatural happened. For starters, his son calmed down and went to sleep. Dad left, the baby slept, and there were no more problems the rest of the night. But just as important, the father felt that the words he had spoken weren't just for his son. God was speaking to *him* as well. He realized that it was God's way of telling him that He was always with him, whether he felt His presence or not. We may not feel like God is there, but He is ever present with us.

FATHER GOD, THANK YOU THAT YOU ARE STILL TAKING CARE OF US, EVEN WHEN IT DOESN'T SEEM LIKE YOU ARE NEAR. PLEASE ASSURE MY FAMILY OF THAT TRUTH SO THAT WE CAN HONOR YOU BY TRUSTING IN YOU.

LEARNING FROM OUR CHILDREN

The wisdom that comes from heaven is first of all pure; then peace-loving, considerate, submissive, full of mercy and good fruit, impartial and sincere.

JAMES 3:17 NIV

Many times, God can use children to soften the hearts of their fathers. As dads, we quickly learn that our children were placed here to *teach* us, at least as much as they were put here to learn from us. Being a dad—especially a dad who cares—is a learning, growing experience.

Bedtime stories are an important ritual in many families. A dad who enjoyed making up stories for his daughters often made the girls the main characters in those stories. He placed his daughters in a setting from the time of Jesus—or King David or another period in history—and created a narrative that not only taught facts about history but conveyed a moral lesson.

One night, after a particularly rough evening with his

children, the dad sat down in their room and told a story as usual—even though he was still hurt and upset by the events that had transpired earlier in the evening. He loved his daughters dearly, but right then he was having trouble liking them. Those emotions played front and center as he told his story. When he finished, one of the girls looked up at him and said, "Dad, that story was about what happened this evening with us, isn't it?" He admitted that it was. Then his daughter stood up, walked over, hugged him, and prayed for him. He wasn't expecting that.

Sometimes dads need teachable moments too. That was one for this dad. In his daughters' actions, he felt that God was speaking to him. *See their love for you? See how your daughters care about you? That's how I want you to approach them.* As dads, we have much wisdom to share with our children. But we must package those lessons with love.

GOD, PLEASE OPEN MY EYES TO SEE WHAT YOU ARE TEACHING ME THROUGH MY CHILDREN. EMPOWER ME TO APPROACH THEM NOT ONLY WITH YOUR WISDOM BUT WITH YOUR LOVE.

WHAT YOU GIVE UP

"If anyone comes to me and does not hate father and mother, wife and children, brothers and sisters— yes, even their own life—such a person cannot be my disciple. And whoever does not carry their cross and follow me cannot be my disciple."

LUKE 14:26–27 NIV

Well, who saw this scripture coming in a dads' devotional? We as Christian men are supposed to *hate* our children. . . in addition to our parents, wives, and siblings?

Clearly, there must be more to Jesus' words than their literal meaning. God's Word is clear that we're all expected to honor our parents. We're supposed to love all people—up to and including our enemies. Children are a gift from God, who should be nurtured and brought up in the knowledge of spiritual things.

So Jesus' words in Luke 14 must be an exaggeration, a dramatic way of teaching some important truth. And the truth is that *God must be our ultimate priority*. Our love for Him should be so strong that our passion for all other people—including our children—seems like hatred.

When we choose to follow Jesus, we become part of God's family. He becomes our heavenly Father whose word is law. As much as we love the kids He's given us, in any conflict between them and God, we take His side. We give up "ownership" to Him, releasing the hopes we've cherished. Why? Because God is the boss.

In His goodness, He may allow your son, for example, to fulfill your dreams of his joining the NFL. But what if God doesn't? What if Junior is simply average? Perhaps even troubled? Can you still love God with the passion He deserves?

This is our calling as Christian dads—to love God with all our heart, soul, mind, and strength, even if (or when) He says no to some dream we have for our kids. They're really His kids anyway. And He may use your submissive obedience to accomplish greater things in their lives.

LORD, I GIVE UP. TAKE MY LIFE— AND MY KIDS' LIVES—AND DO WITH THEM AS YOU SEE FIT.

TAKE MY CAR

Fathers, do not provoke your children,
lest they become discouraged.
Colossians 3:21 esv

A father went through a divorce when his son was young. After custody arrangements were made, the boy became a member of two households with two sets of values. When he started school, he was subjected to yet another set of values. Dad knew that he was competing in some ways for his son's heart, but he always encouraged the boy to show respect for his mom and his teacher and to obey their rules. At the same time, he wanted to build a solid spiritual foundation in his son's life, particularly in those early kindergarten and first-grade years. One day, when the dad was reading a Bible story to his son and seeking to underscore the spiritual lesson, the boy said, "My mom and my teacher said I don't have to believe anything."

Dad was taken aback. At first, he didn't know what to say. But then an idea occurred to him. He fished his car keys out of his pocket and handed them to his son. "Here," he said, "go out and take the car for a drive."

Now it was the boy's turn to be surprised. "Dad," he said, "you know I can't drive. I'm not old enough. I don't know how. And my legs aren't long enough to reach the pedals."

"That's right," his father answered. "You're not old enough. That's why God gave me to you, because there are some things that I know that you don't."

When a child is confrontational, it may be a teachable moment in the making. All we need to do is step back and let God enter the conversation and perform the miracles that only He can perform.

GOD, PLEASE OPEN MY EYES TO SEE THE OPPORTUNITIES IN DISGUISE ALL AROUND ME. WHEN CONVERSATIONS IN MY FAMILY HAVE THE POTENTIAL TO GO BADLY, PLEASE COME NEAR AND TURN THEM AROUND FOR GOOD.

NO DEFENSE

*"Don't you realize that I could ask my Father
for thousands of angels to protect us,
and he would send them instantly?"*
MATTHEW 26:53 NLT

Our experiences as dads can sometimes serve as parables with a deeper meaning. A father was dead tired. His youngest daughter was in bed, but she was miles away from sleep. He was trying to extract himself gracefully by saying all those things fathers say: "Time to go to sleep. No more questions. No more stories." But she wasn't hearing him. Earlier that day, they had been talking about animals and plants. They discussed their natural enemies and how each plant and animal has a means of defense; for example, a cactus has needles and a skunk has a smell. They had talked about tigers and teeth, deer and antlers, chameleons and camouflage. They had pondered how some animals travel in herds or packs to keep themselves safe, whereas some are safer all by themselves, hidden away in the forest. All of this was swimming around in her head, and she needed to talk about it. So she looked her dad in the eye and said, "Daddy, what is the dandelion's defender?"

He was exasperated and wanted to blurt out, "The dandelion has no defender; just go to sleep!" But something stopped him. God was giving him pause. He opened his mouth, and these words came out: "Their defense is producing life. Remember those yellow flowers? Remember how they turn white? Each one of those white puffy pieces is a seed. Each one can make a new dandelion plant. So, no, they don't defend themselves. Instead, they produce life."

What a picture of Jesus Christ! He didn't defend Himself. He could have called an army of angels, but instead, He fell into the hands of evil men. But, by falling, He produced life.

THANK YOU, GOD, FOR THOSE MOMENTS WHEN YOU USE OUR CHILDREN TO TEACH US POWERFUL LESSONS ABOUT LIFE. THANK YOU, JESUS, FOR NOT DEFENDING YOURSELF. THANK YOU FOR GOING TO THE CROSS FOR ME.

MOMENT OF TRUST

To the praise of [God's] glorious grace,
which he has freely given us in the One he loves.
EPHESIANS 1:6 NIV

Many people, dads included, secretly feel that God will never really like them because of the bad things they have done. We may feel too damaged, too tainted, too ruined to ever have a chance with God. For many, unconditional love is such a foreign concept that it doesn't seem real; it doesn't seem possible.

After a dad moved into a new apartment complex, he wanted to be intentional about sharing God's love with his fellow residents. He hosted weekly meals and invited his new friends to attend. One of the families that attended was a young mother with her two small children—one outgoing and the other, a toddler, very shy. The shy child clung to her mother and quickly hid behind her anytime anyone approached. As the dad sat on the floor playing with the other kids, he tried to coax her over to join them but with no success. After several weeks of this, he had all but given up. But one night her shyness seemed to vanish. With a smile on her face and a light in her eye, she waddled over to him, placed something in his hand, and walked away. He looked down. There in his hand was a freshly used tissue.

He did his best to hide his initial reaction. After all, this little girl had finally opened up to him. Then it occurred to him: This is just like coming to Jesus. What do we have to offer? Nothing but our broken lives and the disgusting failure of our sin. But how does He receive us? With open arms. He never turns us away.

GOD, THANK YOU THAT EVEN THOUGH YOU KNOW EVERYTHING THERE IS TO KNOW ABOUT ME, YOU STILL ACCEPT ME AND LOVE ME UNCONDITIONALLY. PLEASE EMPOWER ME TO LOVE MY CHILDREN IN THE SAME WAY.

DON'T WORRY

"Who of you by worrying can add a single hour to your life? Since you cannot do this very little thing, why do you worry about the rest?"
LUKE 12:25–26 NIV

Among parents, moms probably own the greatest reputation as worriers. But let's be honest, dads—don't we worry a bit ourselves? Finances are often at the top of our list of "concerns"...though we also "stress" and "fret" and "stew" over troublesome issues like health (our own and our family's), our careers and sense of personal worth, even the state of our nation and geopolitical affairs. As with any challenge in life, the first step to addressing a problem is to identify it.

So, do you worry? Yes.

Now, how can you fix that?

Earlier in Luke 12, Jesus said point-blank, "Do not worry" (verse 22 NIV). He was prohibiting a debilitating obsession with money, pointing out that greed may be deadly (the parable of the rich fool, verses 13–21) and that God the Father will certainly provide for our physical needs such as food and clothing (verses 22–34). The latter passage is Jesus' beautiful depiction of the birds, who "do not sow or reap. . .yet God feeds them" (verse 24 NIV). And to God, as that verse continues, human beings are far more valuable than birds.

When Jesus makes demands, they are attainable—not in our own strength or goodness, but in God's. Our responsibility is to "seek his kingdom," at which point "these things will be given to you as well" (Luke 12:31 NIV).

Worrying won't help a bit. Will it add a single penny to your bank account? A single minute to a loved one's life? A single point to your kid's batting average? No, no, and no. So why waste your emotional energy?

Consciously and intentionally turn your concerns over to God. You never need to fear when "your Father has been pleased to give you the kingdom" (Luke 12:32 NIV).

FORGIVE ME, FATHER, FOR THE TIMES I WORRY. PLEASE GIVE ME CONFIDENCE IN YOUR WISE AND LOVING PROVISION. I HAVE NO REASON TO FEAR!

DAY 81

RELEASING OUR CHILDREN

*I know the one in whom I trust, and I am sure that
he is able to guard what I have entrusted to him.*
2 TIMOTHY 1:12 NLT

Our children belong to God. Most parents know that in an abstract sense, but learning it in any real way seems to take a long time for many. A dad taught his daughter to ride her bike. When she disappeared around the block, he almost had a fit until he realized that the problem wasn't with her. It was with him. She was growing up, and he couldn't stop it. Another dad thought he trusted God until he dropped his first child off at college. As he was driving home, he found himself pulling over to the side of the road to cry.

It is hard to let go. So much of our God-given role is to be our children's protector. But sometimes we cannot protect them. A father watched as nurses wheeled his six-month-old daughter off to surgery. He focused on her trusting eyes looking at him through the bars of the crib. He felt like a monster. He was letting strangers cut into

168

her body with no guarantee that she would live through the experience. But he had no choice. She needed the operation. He had to open his hands and give her to God.

We do our best to be good fathers to our children. But there are limits to our ability to protect, provide, teach, lead, and love. Fortunately, our heavenly Father has no limits. He knows and loves our children so much more than we do. Though God has given us the privilege of being fathers to our kids, He is their eternal Father, and they are safe with Him. We aren't releasing them to the horrors of this world. We are releasing them to the gentle, loving hands that made them.

GOD, MY CHILDREN BELONG TO YOU. THEY ARE YOURS. IT'S A JOURNEY FOR ME TO LEARN TO COMPLETELY TRUST YOU WITH THEM. BUT I THANK YOU THAT YOU WILL PROTECT WHAT I PUT IN YOUR CARE.

BACK IN THE GAME

"Do not be afraid or discouraged. For the Lord your God is with you wherever you go."
Joshua 1:9 nlt

For one dad, hunting was his passion. For years, he had hunted deer, bear, elk, turkey, and duck. One day, he decided to take his youngest daughter deer hunting for the first time. At the age of thirteen, the experience was all new to her.

Father and daughter were in a blind when a doe started walking near their location. Being inexperienced, the daughter missed several opportunities for a good shot broadside. Then the doe turned and started walking toward them. She was downwind, so it was only a matter of moments before she would pick up the human scent and run. "This is your last chance with this one, sweetie," the dad whispered. The girl took her best shot but missed a dead-center kill shot. The deer was wounded and took off running, leaving a bloody trail for them to follow.

The daughter was excited. She had taken down her

first deer—a rite of passage. But the more they followed the trail, the more doubtful things looked. After a while, all signs of blood disappeared completely. No deer. They circled around and retraced their steps. No deer. Yes, his daughter had definitely wounded the doe, but finding the wounded animal was not to be. What a huge disappointment! The dad knew his daughter had to be crushed. But as he searched for a way to lift her spirits, she gushed with excitement, "Can we come back tomorrow?"

Life is filled with highs and lows, and sometimes they come right next to each other. All of us get knocked down. What makes the difference is how soon we stand up and get back in the game of life.

GOD, HELP US AS A FAMILY TO BE RESILIENT. EMPOWER US TO PERSEVERE. WHEN WE ARE CRUSHED WITH DISAPPOINTMENT, PLEASE COME AND SHOW US THE TRUTH SO THAT WE CAN GET BACK IN THE GAME.

SPACE TO CHOOSE

*In their hearts humans plan their course,
but the LORD establishes their steps.*
PROVERBS 16:9 NIV

We want our kids to do things that are good for them. But too much parental control can suffocate them and push them to rebel later in life. We need to give our children room to make their own choices. For example, a young daughter didn't enjoy math. In the past, her father had tried to convince her to embrace mathematics. "This is something you will want later in life," he kept telling her. But now he gives her more room. "If you want my help," he says, "just let me know." This gives her the freedom to determine if and when she wants help. As a result, she's actually much more open to the help he wants to give.

A young boy was just tall enough to hit his head on the corner of the table. Though tempted to try to protect him, his father didn't rush over to prevent it from happening. Soon, the child banged into the table. It hurt. There were tears. For the next several days he had a bump on his head.

But by refusing to be overly protective, this dad allowed his son to acquire a basic life skill: look where you're going.

Sometimes God takes His hands off our lives to help us realize our need for Him. We may go our own way and bump our heads on the tables of life. Mistakes like alcoholism and sexual irresponsibility hurt. But sometimes God uses our mistakes to show us what was in front of us all along: we need God. God gives us the space we need to freely choose Him.

GOD, THANK YOU FOR GIVING US ROOM TO CHOOSE AND THE FREEDOM TO EXPERIENCE THE CONSEQUENCES OF OUR DECISIONS. GIVE ME WISDOM TO GIVE AN APPROPRIATE AMOUNT OF FREEDOM TO MY CHILDREN.

DAY 84

GOD CARRIES YOU

*"The L*ORD *your God, who is going before you, will fight
for you, as he did for you in Egypt, before your very
eyes, and in the wilderness. There you saw how the
L*ORD *your God carried you, as a father carries his son,
all the way you went until you reached this place."*
DEUTERONOMY 1:30–31 NIV

Is anything better than carrying your young child—a babe
in your arms, a toddler on your hip, or a kindergartner on
your shoulders? You can't carry a child from a distance—by
its very nature, carrying brings two people close together.
It ties one person's strength to another's trust, resulting
in mutual joy. God used this image to describe His relationship with His own children.

To be clear, today's beautiful scripture appears within
a sad, dreary account of Israel's rebellion. Moses was
reminding the people of God's loving leadership as they
journeyed from slavery in Egypt toward their promised
land. But at the last moment, the Israelites balked, terrified
by a report of powerful cities and people in Canaan.

That's when Moses proclaimed, "Do not be terrified; do not be afraid of them" (Deuteronomy 1:29 NIV). Why could the Israelites be confident and unafraid? Because "the LORD your God, who is going before you, will fight for you, as he did for you in Egypt, before your very eyes, and in the wilderness. There you saw how the LORD your God carried you, as a father carries his son, all the way you went until you reached this place."

The Israelites would struggle to trust and obey God for centuries, until they were finally overrun and scattered by powerful enemies. We as Christians, though far from perfect ourselves, have the benefit of God's Spirit living inside us—the Spirit of adoption that allows us to cry, "*Abba,* Father" (Romans 8:15 NIV).

You know how good it is to carry your own child. Now allow God to carry you—in times of pleasure and pain, fear and victory. His strength, your trust, mutual joy.

FATHER GOD, I PLACE MYSELF IN YOUR STRONG HANDS. PLEASE CARRY ME THROUGH EVERY EXPERIENCE, GOOD AND BAD.

STORIES OF TRUTH

Jesus spoke all these things to the crowd in parables; he did not say anything to them without using a parable.
MATTHEW 13:34 NIV

Sometimes we need to see ourselves and our world from a new and different perspective. A dad often told his young children stories at bedtime. Their favorites were tales about a make-believe family of orphans called the Forest Children. Night after night, the four Forest Children experienced one adventure after another as they traveled through the woods under the watchful care of the Great Eagle. They learned how to get along when they wanted to quarrel. They learned relationship skills by dealing with the cantankerous twins, Bert and Norbert, who lived nearby. They laughed at Mr. Slitherslather who ate nothing but candy.

The dad told his children these stories for about two years, until one day his oldest child realized something: "The Forest Children," she said, "they're us, aren't they?

Gabby, Pinball, D, and Suzie—those are just other names for us!" She was right, of course. All along he had been telling them about themselves, trying to help them see their world through a different set of eyes.

Stories are a wonderful way of teaching children, because kids tend to remember the plot and the characters for a long time. Later, when they're ready, they will begin to comprehend and appreciate the lessons behind the stories. It's no surprise that God used parables and simple stories to teach His people. Jesus, the master storyteller, used stories to explain many things, including how faith works, why some people follow God and others don't, and how God feels when people come back to Him.

Why stories? Jesus explained that, as well. Stories are like birthday presents. When the time is right, we can take off the wrapping and discover God's truth inside.

GOD, THANK YOU FOR PACKAGING WHAT I NEED TO KNOW IN A WAY THAT I CAN REMEMBER. OPEN MY EYES AT THE RIGHT TIME SO THAT I CAN SEE WHAT I NEED TO SEE. EMPOWER ME TO TEACH MY CHILDREN IN WAYS THEY WILL LONG REMEMBER.

POWER STRUGGLES

A servant of the Lord must not quarrel but must be kind to everyone, be able to teach, and be patient with difficult people.

2 TIMOTHY 2:24 NLT

We can avoid power struggles with our children by not turning everything into a battle. For example, a dad used to insist that his kids eat their vegetables. Then one day he realized that his wife didn't eat vegetables. He was the only one in the house who did. A voice inside seemed to be saying, *Let it go.*

In another instance, the dad's daughter wrote some of her own songs. Anxious to preserve them, he arranged for a recording session in their home. But his daughter refused to cooperate. When the time came for her to sing, she was slouched over. "Stand up and sing," he said to her. But no, she wanted to sing slouched over. This conflict brought the recording session to an end. After that experience, he decided he didn't want to deprive his daughter of the joy of songwriting just because he was focused on preserving her work. The voice inside had said, *Let it go.* So he did.

A boy refused to do his homework. Every night was a power struggle. His dad met with his teachers. He tried every parenting trick he knew, but getting even one math problem done was like pulling teeth. What made it even more frustrating was that his son was a walking encyclopedia. He probably knew more history than his teacher, but he was getting a D-minus in the class. Finally, the dad just let go. A year later, his son was getting almost straight As because he was enrolled in welding, construction, and hands-on courses. Dad realized, *This is a good thing. He knows what he likes.*

Some battles are worth fighting. Some are not. We look to God for the wisdom to tell the difference.

GOD, PLEASE GIVE ME WISDOM AS I DEAL WITH MY CHILDREN. HELP ME TO AVOID POWER STRUGGLES WITH THEM. LET ME NOT BATTLE WITH THEM OVER THINGS THAT AREN'T THAT IMPORTANT.

A SENSE OF WONDER

*As the waters fill the sea, the earth will be filled
with an awareness of the glory of the Lord.*
HABAKKUK 2:14 NLT

Often, one of the casualties of growing up is that we lose our sense of wonder. We become sophisticated, even jaded. We've seen it all, done it all, and nothing impresses us anymore. This is a great loss because it impedes our ability to appreciate God and the beauty that is so connected with Him.

As dads, we have the great privilege of rediscovering our world each day through the eyes of our children. A little baby discovers her fingers for the first time. A trip to the zoo or the aquarium becomes a voyage of wonder. Getting stuck waiting at a railroad crossing becomes an opportunity to play "Count the Cars."

A dad was at a professional baseball game with his young son. The boy—apparently a civil engineer in the making—looked around the covered stadium and said with excitement, "Dad, this is one big room made out of metal and concrete!"

What are our children teaching us? They teach us to see the same old things through new eyes. They teach us that a grasshopper is a marvel, blowing bubbles and watching them float away is great fun, and clouds are works of art. They teach us to slow down, to stop and see what we can't see when we're traveling 100 miles an hour through our adult world.

Jesus taught us that to find God we must become like children. No wonder the enemy of our souls works so hard to keep us caught up in the complicated and hurried affairs of life. The eyes of a child help us discover the fingerprints of God in our world.

GOD, THANK YOU FOR WHAT YOU ARE TEACHING ME THROUGH MY CHILDREN. OPEN MY EYES TO SEE WHAT THEY SEE. KEEP ME FROM BEING JADED. RESTORE A SENSE OF WONDER INSIDE ME SO THAT I CAN WORSHIP YOU.

DAY 88

ANYTIME, ANYWHERE

*Love the L*ORD *your God with all your heart and
with all your soul and with all your strength.
These commandments that I give you today
are to be on your hearts. Impress them on
your children. Talk about them when you sit
at home and when you walk along the road,
when you lie down and when you get up.*

DEUTERONOMY 6:5–7 NIV

Do you have family devotions? Do your kids look forward
to set Bible times with you? Are they learning theologi-
cal concepts, memorizing scriptures, growing deeper in
relationship to God? If so, great—thank God for such a
positive, upbeat spiritual experience with your children.

Not every home is like that, no matter how hard the
parents may try. Some kids are, shall we say, *active*. They're
easily distracted. They're hard to pin down. And even
though Mom and Dad would love to have a systematic
Bible time with their kids, that might require a miracle
on the order of Creation.

You folks in the peaceful, easy homes, please don't judge. Y'all in the vortex, don't envy. God knew what He was doing when He gave you your kids. And however yours are wired, God has ways of getting through to them.

If they like to sit and listen and learn, your job is relatively easy. For the busy, busy, busy crowd, Deuteronomy 6 offers some wise instruction: teach your kids about God anytime, anywhere. If they won't sit for a prepared lesson, just talk as you walk, as you sit, as you lay them down and get them up. Of course, the message will carry greater weight if you, Dad, "love the LORD your God with all your heart and with all your soul and with all your strength."

Dads of easy kids need to love God that way too. And they can also talk to their kids about the Lord anytime, anywhere.

Being a Christian never stops. Neither does being a Christian dad.

HELP ME, FATHER, TO BE THE EXACT KIND OF DAD MY KIDS NEED.

THE PATH TO GROWTH

*Who are you to condemn someone else's
servants? Their own master will judge whether
they stand or fall. And with the Lord's help,
they will stand and receive his approval.*

ROMANS 14:4 NLT

For many years, a young boy couldn't read. Though some
kids were starting to read at age four, he wasn't interested.
Alphabet and phonics lessons at six and seven didn't stick.
His dad wasn't overly concerned. Many kids, especially
boys, start reading late. The family was homeschooling, so
he wasn't at risk for teasing or bullying. The boy's parents
didn't make an issue of the boy's late development, until
at age eight when the boy brought it up.

Walking through the library in search of some books
one day, he said, "Dad, it really bothers me that I can't read."
His dad told him the story of Albert Einstein, of how he
got a slow start, but that didn't help much. The boy's pain
intensified as he got further involved in the kids' program
at church. It was workbook intensive, and it was painfully

obvious that he was the only one in class who couldn't read a word of it. Every Wednesday night he would get a stomachache and beg not to go.

At age ten, the boy still wasn't recognizing the letters of the alphabet. His dad took him to a specialist for neurological testing. In the midst of that six-month evaluation period, something miraculous happened. Around age eleven, the alphabet started making sense. Phonics started to work for him. By age thirteen, he was reading at grade level. Now he's a college student with an above-average IQ, who reads constantly, illustrating that people master skills at different times and in different ways.

God doesn't pigeonhole people. He lets people grow in different ways. Each person's spiritual journey is unique. Just as this young man learned to read when he was ready to read, so also each person will grow when they're ready.

GOD, GRANT ME THE PATIENCE TO LET MY CHILDREN GROW THE WAY THEY WERE DESIGNED TO GROW. ALLOW ME TO APPRECIATE THE DIVERSITY OF PEOPLE AROUND ME WITHOUT TRYING TO SQUEEZE OTHERS INTO THE MOLD OF MY EXPECTATIONS.

DAY 90

ETERNALLY RELEVANT

*Jesus Christ is the same yesterday
and today and forever.*
HEBREWS 13:8 NIV

Sitting with a group of teens, one dad noticed that they were all cradling their phones in their hands, texting away. "Hey, did you hear," he said to the group, "they've come out with a new cellular technology. It's where you use your voice."

"You mean voice to text?" one of the girls asked him, clearly thinking there was no way this old man could be more tech savvy than she was.

"Even better," he said with a smile. "Voice to voice."

She looked at him, confused, for a long moment and then went back to texting.

There will always be differences between generations. People who are part of the Baby Boom generation experienced generational issues with their parents' generation, the Builders, the people who survived the Great Depression and World War II. Builders could never figure out Boomers' endless obsession with "finding themselves." For most Builders, it never mattered whether a person liked his job or hated it—one should choose the job that paid the most, because that's what work was for: earning money. To Boomers, that was ridiculous. Why would you spend your life doing something that "wasn't you"?

Our children will be children of their generation. They will absorb many of the values, perspectives, and practices of others their own age. That is unavoidable. But it is also an opportunity. We can learn from them. We can encourage them in the strengths of their generation's point of view and fortify them in those areas where we offer a stronger perspective. Most of all, we can remind our children and ourselves that—regardless of passing fads and customs—our unchanging God remains eternally relevant.

THANK YOU, GOD, THAT YOU REMAIN THE SAME YESTERDAY, TODAY, AND FOREVER. PLEASE HELP ME TO SEE AND COMMUNICATE TO MY CHILDREN HOW RELEVANT YOU ARE TO EVERY PART OF OUR LIVES.

STANDING
AGAINST THE FOE

Be strong in the Lord and in his mighty power.
EPHESIANS 6:10 NIV

While bow hunting for bear in northern Manitoba, a hunter first encountered "Scarface." While he was working a bait, about ten different bears came and went. But he didn't want just any bear; he wanted a trophy—a twenty-inch skull. Unfortunately, he was shooting video instead of arrows when two boars came through, following a sow in heat. By the time he realized he had just seen a seven-foot black bear, it was too late. The animal was out of range. As the hunt drew to a close, he was forced to settle for a lesser animal. But he had no sooner killed the smaller bear when Scarface, the seven-foot bear, showed up again. Before the man could get to his kill, Scarface grabbed up the smaller animal with his massive jaws and dragged him deep into the undergrowth.

In the gathering darkness, the hunter wondered what he

should do. His preferred trophy was right in front of him, but he couldn't shoot it. He had only one tag, and Scarface was busy tearing that bear apart. He had no choice. He had to run him off, but that was easier said than done.

The hunter charged. Scarface retreated then stopped, turned around, and started walking back toward the man. The hunter charged again. Same response. This happened five times before the bear finally backed down and wandered off.

As dads, it's our job to take a stand against everything that would like to tear apart our families. How we do that varies depending on the situation, but God will give us the courage and confidence to prevail.

By the way, the hunter returned to Manitoba every year. Finally, after a couple of years, he tracked down Scarface and shot him. He got his trophy bear.

GOD, GRANT ME THE STRENGTH, WISDOM, AND COURAGE TO FIGHT AGAINST THE THINGS THAT FIGHT AGAINST MY FAMILY. THANK YOU FOR PROVIDING THE ARMOR AND RESOURCES I NEED TO PREVAIL.

SPEAK TRUTH

When the time drew near for David to die,
he gave a charge to Solomon his son. "I am about
to go the way of all the earth," he said. "So be
strong, act like a man, and observe what the
LORD your God requires: Walk in obedience to
him, and keep his decrees and commands."
1 KINGS 2:1–3 NIV

A man struggled to connect with his teenage daughter. His attempts at conversation usually ended quickly, with the girl stomping away in a huff.

One night, driving her home from after-school practice, dad broached a topic that was troubling him: her boyfriend.

"I think you can do better," he told his daughter. "Why do you say that?" she snorted. Dad breathed a quick, silent prayer, and elaborated. The girl wasn't happy, but she didn't argue, at least.

A month later, she broke up with the boy. And when asked why, the girl repeated dad's arguments almost point for point. Not surprisingly, she didn't *credit* dad...but he didn't mind. Somehow, she'd heard the truth he spoke and then acted on it.

As fathers, we're not guaranteed good results from our teaching. But we are fully expected to speak the truth—biblical, practical, and observational—to our kids. Then we pray that God will sink that truth into their hearts and improve their lives.

In today's scripture, David shared some vitally important truth with his son Solomon. As Israel's greatest king sensed his death nearing, these were essentially "famous last words." Though you'd think the somberness of the moment would have had a mighty impression on Solomon, he later crashed and burned, morally and spiritually. And yet the book of Ecclesiastes seems to indicate that he returned to his humble faith—what his father taught him—late in life.

It isn't always easy to speak truth to our kids. But the Christian life wasn't intended to be easy. What truth do your kids need to hear from you today? What keeps you from speaking it?

LORD JESUS, YOU ARE THE TRUTH. HELP ME TO SPEAK YOUR TRUTH TO MY CHILD.

OVERCOMING DISCOURAGEMENT

No, in all these things we are more than conquerors through him who loved us.
ROMANS 8:37 NIV

When our kids experience discouragement, it can help to ponder what others have overcome. Beethoven's teacher considered him hopeless as a composer. Bob Dylan's band lost a high school talent competition. Thomas Edison's teachers told him he was "too stupid to learn anything." Albert Einstein didn't even speak until he was four. His teacher called him "mentally slow." A movie producer told actor Harrison Ford that he would probably never succeed. Henry Ford went out of business three times before becoming one of the greatest entrepreneurs in American history. Stephen King threw his first novel in the trash. *M*A*S*H* was rejected by twenty-one publishers before becoming a bestselling book, a huge movie hit, and one of the longest-running television series of all time.

Douglas MacArthur was twice refused admission to West Point. He got in on the third try and became one of the most successful generals of World War II. Marilyn Monroe was told she wasn't pretty or talented enough to be an actress. Babe Ruth held the record for most baseball strikeouts. Before he founded KFC, Colonel Sanders went out of business at an age when most people were retiring. Twenty-seven publishers rejected the first book by Dr. Seuss. Vincent van Gogh sold only one painting in his entire life—not to a customer but to a friend. Oprah Winfrey lost her job as a television reporter because "she wasn't fit to be on screen."

Our failures don't define us. The opinions of others don't count for much. Only one opinion matters: God's. And He chose us and our children to be part of His family forever. Do we have what it takes? Of course we do. We have the best Dad in the universe, and He is determined to coach us to success.

THANK YOU, GOD, FOR LIFTING US UP WHEN WE FEEL DISCOURAGED. THANK YOU THAT YOU HAVE A PERFECT PLAN FOR MY CHILDREN AND THAT YOU ARE COACHING ALL OF US, EMPOWERING US TO SUCCEED.

GIVING ALL TO PROVIDE

"For this is how God loved the world: He gave his one and only Son, so that everyone who believes in him will not perish but have eternal life."

JOHN 3:16 NLT

Boxer Billy Miske made his living in the ring. He was good at what he did—almost good enough to be a national champion. In fact, the only losses in his 48–2–2 record were to two champions. One of those losses was to world heavyweight champion Jack Dempsey, considered one of the best boxers of all time.

But Miske carried with him a secret that none of his opponents, none of his promoters—not even his wife— knew. He was terminally ill with kidney disease. His doctor had ordered him to retire from the ring. But times were tough, and his family was depending on him to provide for them financially. So even though he was so sick that he could hardly walk, let alone train, he convinced his promoters to schedule a final fight. Amazingly, he not only survived the fight, but he knocked out his young challenger in the fourth round. He took the purse, $2,400, and bought a piano for his wife, toys for his kids, and the furniture he had pawned earlier to survive.

A week later, he was dead at the age of twenty-nine.

Many dads have given everything to provide for their families. They've worked long hours at jobs they hate, often for little pay, enduring abuse at the hands of supervisors and coworkers. Many of these dads do what they do without complaint. It's part of the territory.

Our Father in heaven spent everything He had to provide for His children. He saw that we couldn't provide a way out of our sin and back to Him on our own. He gave what cost Him the most, His only Son, Jesus, to die on the cross on our behalf to provide a way for us to have eternal life.

THANK YOU, FATHER IN HEAVEN, FOR GIVING YOUR SON TO PROVIDE A WAY FOR US TO BE FORGIVEN AND RECEIVED INTO HEAVEN TO LIVE FOREVER WITH YOU. JESUS, I GIVE MY LIFE AND MY FAMILY TO YOU.

A NIGHT OF PEACE

*While we were God's enemies, we were reconciled
to him through the death of his Son.*
ROMANS 5:10 NIV

On Christmas Eve 1944, during the Battle of the Bulge, a mother and her twelve-year-old son were preparing a Christmas meal in a small cottage just inside Germany when a knock came on the door. When the woman answered the door, she was greeted by three American soldiers. They were the enemy, but she noticed that one of them was badly wounded.

"Come in," she said in German. The men were nearly frozen to death. In the confusion of battle, they had become separated from their comrades and had been wandering for three days in the forest. The woman and her son got busy, bandaging wounds and putting together a meal.

Then there came a second knock on the door. This time four soldiers stood there—Germans. Even though the woman knew she could be shot, she told the newcomers they were welcome to spend the night but that she had other guests they would not consider friends. Then, in a firm voice, she told them, "This is Christmas Eve, and there will be no shooting here." Somehow she convinced all the soldiers to turn their weapons over to her. Then they shared a meal. The German medic aided the wounded American, and all nine people in the house spent the night in peace. In the morning, the soldiers directed one another back to their lines.

Making peace is not always easy, comfortable, or convenient. But as leaders of our families, sometimes we need to step into explosive situations and act with great courage. The future may depend on our ability to de-escalate conflicts and bring hurt and offended people back into relationship. We take our lead from Jesus, who brought the enemies of God back into relationship with Him.

GOD, ONLY YOU CAN BRING LASTING PEACE. AS A DAD, I DEPEND ON YOU TO BRING YOUR PRESENCE INTO OUR FAMILY SO THAT HURTS CAN BE HEALED AND DIFFERENCES CAN BE RESOLVED. EMPOWER US AS A FAMILY TO BE INSTRUMENTS OF YOUR PEACE.

DISCIPLINE

*My son, do not despise the LORD's discipline, and do
not resent his rebuke, because the LORD disciplines
those he loves, as a father the son he delights in.*
PROVERBS 3:11–12 NIV

As with so many words in the English language, *discipline*
carries multiple meanings. The term can refer to correction and punishment. It can also imply the self-control
gained by an orderly pattern of conduct and behavior.
Christian dads know that their kids need both aspects
in their lives.

The discipline mentioned in Proverbs 3:11–12 is of
the first sort. A rebuke is a form of correction—a sharp
reprimand that says, "You're doing this wrong and you
need to change your ways." Dads know that their kids
occasionally need this kind of firm redirection—because
we all know that *we* needed it (and sometimes still do
need it) ourselves.

The other type of discipline is self-control, mentioned
in the famous "fruit of the Spirit" passage of Galatians

5:22–23. Now, just as a reminder: we're not saved by any good works we do, including any self-imposed limitations on our needs or wants. But once we are saved—by God's grace, through our faith in Jesus—good works should inevitably follow in the process of sanctification, our growth in grace. Through our Bible reading and prayer and self-denial and service, we discipline ourselves to be more like our Lord Himself.

Christian dads should long to see their kids exhibiting this kind of discipline. But let's be honest with ourselves: Do they see self-discipline in our lives? Is it obvious that we ourselves are truly working to better reflect Jesus' life and teaching?

An example is a powerful thing. For the sake of our kids—and our entire world—let's make sure our example is as consistently good as it can be.

HEAVENLY FATHER, YOU HAVE OFTEN DISCIPLINED ME FOR MY BENEFIT. PLEASE HELP ME TO WISELY DISCIPLINE MY KIDS—AND TO SET AN EXAMPLE OF SELF—DISCIPLINE THAT THEY'LL BE INCLINED TO FOLLOW.

DAY 97

TAKING A STAND

The eyes of the LORD range throughout
the earth to strengthen those whose
hearts are fully committed to him.
2 CHRONICLES 16:9 NIV

The year 1951 was a magical one for the University of San Francisco. The school wasn't known for its football team, but that year the right combination of talent and coaching came together, and the team finished the year undefeated with a 9–0–0 record.

Hours after the San Francisco Dons won their final game, Orange Bowl officials invited the team to play. It was a dream come true. Playing in a bowl game would make it much easier for the team's players to have a shot at a professional career in football. In addition, the university stood to gain the financial backing it needed for its struggling football program.

But 1951 was also the height of the Jim Crow era in the South. African Americans were not welcome as equal participants in the white-dominated Southern culture.

The bowl invitation arrived with a condition. Burl Toler and Ollie Matson, the two black members of the team, were not welcome. Knowing full well what it would cost, every member of the team turned down the invitation. The football program didn't receive the funding it needed, and it never really recovered. But several members of the team went on to play pro football; three members, including Matson, were inducted into football's Hall of Fame. In 2006, surviving members of the 1951 team were at the university's graduation ceremonies receiving honorary doctorates. All three thousand people present rose to their feet to give them a long standing ovation for their act of courage taken fifty-five years earlier.

There will always be forces seeking to sway our children to compromise their values and do something other than the right thing. As dads, we lead the way, teaching our children to stand up for what is right, even when everyone stands against them.

GOD, PLEASE GRANT MY CHILDREN AND ME THE COURAGE WE NEED TO STAND FOR WHAT IS RIGHT, EVEN WHEN OUR STAND IS NOT POPULAR OR ACCEPTED. GIVE US THE WISDOM TO UNDERSTAND THE TIMES AND TO KNOW WHICH CHOICE IS BEST.

THAT'S EXASPERATING!

*Children, obey your parents in the Lord,
for this is right. "Honor your father and mother"—
which is the first commandment with a promise—
"so that it may go well with you and that you
may enjoy long life on the earth." Fathers, do not
exasperate your children; instead, bring them
up in the training and instruction of the Lord.*

Ephesians 6:1–4 niv

In the relationship between fathers and children, nobody gets a free pass.

The kids' duty goes all the way back to the Ten Commandments. "Honor your father and your mother" (Exodus 20:12 NIV) is the fifth commandment, the first one that addresses our human relationships. In Ephesians, the apostle Paul noted that this commandment came with a promise of well-being. When kids obey their parents, the entire household benefits.

But dads have an obligation too—they are never to

"exasperate" their kids. Several other translations—including the English Standard Version, the New Living Translation, and the New American Standard Bible—say, "Do not provoke your children to anger." Why would a dad want to do that? Well, maybe he doesn't want to, but if the kids aren't keeping up their end of the bargain, a father might react in such a way as to exasperate his children.

Yes, fathers are the head of the home. Yes, they reflect the fatherhood of God and should be treated appropriately. But there will be times when your kids—sinful creatures that they are—disrespect and disobey you. And now you have a choice to make: Will you respect and obey your heavenly Father and do what He says in His Word? Or will you lash out in frustration and provoke your kids to anger?

Kids will be kids. But you're the adult here. Why not pray right now to respond properly the next time your kids exasperate you.

HEAVENLY FATHER, THANKS FOR YOUR PATIENCE WITH ME. PLEASE PREPARE MY HEART FOR THOSE TOUGH TIMES WITH THE KIDS SO THAT I WILL RESPOND APPROPRIATELY AND NOT EXASPERATE THEM.

DAY 99

HOW COULD WE DO LESS?

Arise, cry out in the night, as the watches of the night begin; pour out your heart like water in the presence of the Lord. Lift up your hands to him for the lives of your children, who faint from hunger at every street corner.

LAMENTATIONS 2:19 NIV

Lamentations seems like a strange place to seek advice for fatherhood. This little book, squeezed into scripture between the long prophecies of Jeremiah and Ezekiel, oozes with despair. It paints a dreary picture of sin's consequences—the figurative death of rebellious Judah and the literal death of many of her people.

And yet in the midst of horrendous scenes of pain and sadness, we see a reminder to pray for our children.

The author, presumably Jeremiah, had witnessed tragedies that few people alive today ever have. We as Christian dads can hope that the kind of judgments that fell on Judah never come near our homes.

But isn't that all the more reason for us to be praying—regularly and earnestly—for our children? As followers of

Jesus, we have been blessed "with every spiritual blessing in Christ" (Ephesians 1:3 NIV). Most of us live in free and prosperous places where the life-threatening trauma Jeremiah witnessed is almost unthinkable. Out of gratitude and obligation to God, why wouldn't we lift up our hands to Him for the physical, emotional, and spiritual lives of our kids?

Dads, let's follow the example of Israel's great prophet Samuel. Toward the end of his life, passing along final words of wisdom to his people, he said, "Far be it from me that I should sin against the LORD by failing to pray for you" (1 Samuel 12:23 NIV).

As fathers of children given to us by God Himself—as the stewards of one of His greatest gifts—how could we do less?

THANK YOU, LORD, FOR THE CHILDREN YOU'VE GIVEN ME. PLEASE HELP ME TO PRAY CONSISTENTLY FOR THEIR PHYSICAL, EMOTIONAL, AND SPIRITUAL WELL-BEING. I ASK FOR YOUR GREATEST BLESSINGS TO BE UPON THEM.

ALL THINGS TO MY KIDS

To the weak I became weak, to win the weak.
I have become all things to all people so that
by all possible means I might save some.
1 CORINTHIANS 9:22 NIV

Our greatest goal for our children cannot be worldly success. A father's highest aspiration must be that his kids know and follow Jesus.

Of course, children who truly serve the Lord will become "successful" in the sense of making better life choices, working hard, and getting along with others—including their parents. But if we emphasize our kids' income, connections, and pleasure over their relationship with God, we all lose in the end.

That's why Christian dads should follow the apostle Paul's example. His goal was to see people—Jews and Gentiles alike—being saved. And he made himself "a slave to everyone, to win as many as possible" (1 Corinthians 9:19 NIV).

Paul meant that "to the Jews I became like a Jew, to win

the Jews. To those under the law I became like one under the law (though I myself am not under the law), so as to win those under the law. To those not having the law I became like one not having the law (though I am not free from God's law but under Christ's law), so as to win those not having the law" (1 Corinthians 9:20–21 NIV). Then he completed his thought with the words of the scripture above.

What are the "all things" we can become to our kids so that by all possible means we might save some? Do we need to show more interest in their music, their video games, their social media? Do we need to get off the couch and kick a soccer ball, throw a baseball, or bump a volleyball? Do we need to join them in baking, painting, or fixing a bike?

This isn't coddling, it's connecting. It's an attempt to meet your kids where they are so that you can all share in the most important thing of all: salvation through Jesus Christ.

LORD, PLEASE GIVE ME WISDOM AND STRENGTH TO BE EXACTLY WHAT MY KIDS NEED ME TO BE.